DASH DIET
COOKBOOK
FOR BEGINNERS

1500-Day Easy & Delicious Low Sodium Recipes to Lower Your Blood Pressure &
Healthy Weight Loss. Live Healthier without Sacrificing Taste.
Includes 30-Day Meal Plan

Melissa Jordon

MELISSA JORDON
— collection —

DOWNLOAD YOUR GIFT NOW!

The bonus is **100% FREE**.
You don't need to enter any details except your name and email address.

To download your bonus scan the QR code below or go to

https://melissajordon.me/bonus/

SCAN ME

ANTI-INFLAMMATORY Cookbook for Beginners

1200 Day Recipes to Improve Your Health, Reduce Inflammation and Lose Weight

Table of Contents

Introduction 11

    What is dash Diet? 11

    What to eat and what to avoid in DASH diet 13

    Shopping List 15

Chapter 1: Breakfasts 16

    1.   Vegetarian Breakfast Salad with Eggs 16

    2.   Cheesy Egg in Avocado 16

    3.   Bulgur Breakfast with Fruits 16

    4.   Quinoa Breakfast Bowls 17

    5.   Marinara Poached Eggs 17

    6.   Low Carb Green Smoothie 17

    7.   Fig with Ricotta Oatmeal 18

    8.   Grilled Basil Lemon Tofu Burgers 18

    9.   Smoked Salmon Avocado Toast 19

    10.   Delicious Fluffy Almond Flour Pancakes 19

    11.   Mediterranean Breakfast Eggs 19

    12.   Morning Overnight Oats with Raspberries 20

    13.   Morning Mediterranean Frittata 20

    14.   Dried Cranberries Cinnamon Oatmeal 21

    15.   Corn Banana Fritters 21

    16.   Healthy Avocado Smoothie 22

    17.   Simple Apple Tahini Toast 22

    18.   Savory Breakfast Oatmeal 22

    19.   Baked Avocado Eggs 22

    20.   Easy Berry and Nut Parfait 23

Chapter 2: Salads and Sides 24

    21.   Rainbow Slaw 24

    22.   Dash Diet Waldorf Salad 24

    23.   Shrimp & Nectarine Salad 24

    24.   Roasted Sweet Potato & Chickpea Pitas 25

    25.   Strawberry-Blue Cheese Steak Salad 25

    26.   Turkey Medallions with Tomato Salad 26

27. Warm Rice and Pinto Salad 26

28. Grilled Southwestern Steak Salad 27

29. Thai-Style Cobb Salad 28

30. Cherry-Chicken Lettuce Wraps 28

31. Lentil Medley 28

32. Spicy Almonds 29

33. Italian Sausage-Stuffed Zucchini 29

34. Chickpea Mint Tabbouleh 30

35. Pesto Corn Salad with Shrimp 30

36. Southwest Shredded Pork Salad 31

37. Edamame Salad with Sesame Ginger Dressing 31

38. Cilantro Lime Shrimp 32

39. Sardines with Lemony Tomato Sauce 32

40. Baby Potato and Olive Salad 32

Chapter 3: Sauces, Dips, and Dressings 34

41. Asparagus with Horseradish Dip 34

42. Layered Hummus Dip 34

43. Skinny Quinoa Veggie Dip 34

44. Dill Dip 35

45. Low Sodium Spaghetti Sauce 35

46. Avocado Dip 35

47. Avocado Salsa 36

48. Cilantro Lime Dressing 36

49. House Ranch Dressing 36

50. Italian Salad Dressing 36

51. Mango Salsa 37

52. Peach Honey Spread 37

53. Peanut Butter Hummus 37

54. Pepper Sauce 37

55. Savory Vegetable Dip 38

56. Vegetable salsa 38

57. Mushroom Sauce 38

58. Spinach Dip with Mushrooms 39

59. Blue Cheese Dressing 39

60. Cilantro Lime Dressing 39

Chapter 4: Beans and Grains 40

61. Mexican Bake 40

62. Cannellini Bean Hummus 40

63. Black Bean & White Cheddar Frittata 40

64. Black Bean & Sweet Potato Rice Bowls 41

65. White Beans & Bow Ties 41

66. Black Bean and Corn Relish 42

67. Gluten-Free Hummus 42

68. Hummus 43

69. Peanut Butter Hummus 43

70. White Bean Dip 43

71. Bean Salad with Balsamic Vinaigrette 44

72. Whole-Grain Pancakes 44

73. Quick Bean and Tuna Salad 44

74. Rice and Beans Salad 45

75. Black Bean Wrap 45

76. Hot 6-Grain Cereal 46

77. Turkish Canned Pinto Bean Salad 46

78. Shrimp with Black Bean Pasta 47

79. Rustic Lentil and Basmati Rice Pilaf 47

80. Quick Spanish Rice 47

Chapter 5: Vegetarian Recipes 49

81. Minestrone Soup 49

82. Swiss Chard Egg Drop Soup 49

83. Roasted Veggies and Brown Rice Bowl 49

84. Creamy Cauliflower Chickpea Curry 50

85. Stuffed Portobello Mushrooms with Spinach 51

86. Veggie-Stuffed Portobello Mushrooms 51

87. Cauliflower Hash with Carrots 52

88. Garlicky Zucchini Cubes with Mint 52

89. Zucchini and Artichokes Bowl with Farro 52

90. Zucchini Fritters 53

91. Moroccan Tagine with Vegetables 53

92. Acorn squash with Apples 54

93. Asparagus with Hazelnut Gremolata 54

94. Baked Apples with Cherries and Almonds 55

95. Braised Celery Root 55

96. Braised Kale with Cherry Tomatoes 56

97. Baby Minted Carrots 56

98. Broccoli with Garlic and Lemon 57

99. Cauliflower Mashed 'Potatoes' 57

100.   Cheesy Baked Zucchini 57

Chapter 6: Vegan Recipes 59

101.   Grilled Vegetable Sewers 59

102.   Honey Sage Carrots 59

103.   Wilted Dandelion Greens with Sweet Onion 59

104.   Lentil Ragout 60

105.   Celery and Mustard Greens 60

106.   Potato Salad 60

107.   Vegetable and Tofu Scramble 61

108.   Chinese Style Asparagus 61

109.   Zoodles 61

110.   Creole Style Black Eyed Peas 62

111.   Sweet Pepper Stew 62

112.   Eggplant with Toasted Spices 63

113.   Vegetable and Red Lentil Stew 63

114.   Glazed Root Vegetable 64

115.   Cauliflower Steaks with Arugula 64

116.   Green Beans with Red Pepper and Garlic 64

117.   Grilled Romaine Lettuce 65

118.   Brussels sprouts with Shallots and Lemon 65

119.   Chickpea Lettuce Wraps with Celery 66

120.   Stir Fried Eggplant 66

Chapter 7: Fish and Seafood 68

121.   Mediterranean Baked Fish 68

122.   Sea Food Corn Chowder 68

123.   Salmon with Horseradish Pistachio Crust 69

124.   Crab Cake Egg Stacks 69

125.   Crunchy Baked Fish 70

126.   Prawns Puttanesca 70

127.   Quick Bean and Tuna Salad 71

128.   Quinoa Risotto with Arugula and Parmesan 71

129.   Roasted Salmon 72

130.   Roasted Salmon with Maple Glaze 72

131.   Seasoned Baked Cod 73

132.   Baked Lemon Salmon 73

133.   Baked Salmon with Basil and Tomato 73

134.   Honey-Mustard Roasted Salmon 74

135.   Salmon and Mushroom Hash with Pesto 74

136.   Spiced Citrus Sole 75

137.   Crispy Tilapia with Mango Salsa 75

138.   Mediterranean Grilled Sea Bass 76

139.   Baked Halibut Steaks with Vegetables 76

140.   Spicy Haddock Stew 77

Chapter 8: Meat Recipes: Meat, Pork, Lamb, Poultry 78

141.   Asian Pork Tenderloin 78

142.   Baked chicken and Wild Rice 78

143.   Grilled Lemon Chicken 79

144.   Quick Chicken Salad Wraps 79

145.   Roasted Chicken Thighs With Basmati Rice 80

146.   Herbed-Mustard-Coated Pork Tenderloin 80

147.   Grilled Chicken and Zucchini Kebabs 81

148.   Macadamia Pork 81

149.   Almond-Crusted Chicken Tenders with Honey 82

150.   Parsley-Dijon Chicken and Potatoes 82

151.   Gyro Burgers with Tahini Sauce 83

152.   Greek-Style Lamb Burgers 84

153. Crispy Pesto Chicken 84

154. Roasted Pork Tenderloin 85

155. Lamb Kofta (Spiced Meatballs) 85

156. Beef and Vegetable Kebabs 86

157. Spiced Roast Chicken 86

158. Coconut Chicken Tenders 87

159. Beef stroganoff 87

160. Five-spice pork medallions 88

Chapter 9: Stews and Soups 90

161. Beef, Tomato, and Lentils Stew 90

162. Potato Lamb and Olive Stew 90

163. Slow Cook Lamb Shanks with Cannellini Beans Stew 91

164. Beef Stew with Beans and Zucchini 91

165. Beef Stew with Fennel and Shallots 92

166. Beef and Vegetable Stew 93

167. Tuscan White Bean Stew 93

168. Vegetable, Lentil and Garbanzo Bean Stew 94

169. Sweet Pepper Stew 95

170. Vegetable and Red Lentil Stew 95

171. Mediterranean Tomato Hummus Soup 96

172. Avgolemono (Lemon Chicken Soup) 96

173. Vegetable Fagioli Soup Sugar 97

174. Chicken and Pastina Soup 97

175. Mushroom Barley Soup 98

176. Greens, Fennel, and Pear Soup with Cashews 98

177. Moroccan Lentil, Tomato, and Cauliflower Soup 99

178. Carrot Soup 99

179. Curried Cream of Tomato Soup with Apples 100

180. Home-Style Turkey Soup 100

Chapter 10: Desserts 102

181. Healthy Chocolate Chip Cookies 102

182. Sugar Cookie 102

183. Strawberries with Peppered Balsamic Drizzle 103

184. Vanilla Chia Seed Pudding Toppings..103

185. Mango Banana Soft Serve...103

186. Almond and Apricot Biscotti...104

187. Ambrosia with Coconut and Toasted Almonds 104

188. Fruitcake 105

189. Strawberries and Cream Cheese Crepes...105

190. Strawberry Shortcake..106

191. Soft Chocolate Cake..106

192. Banana Cranberry and Oat Bars 107

193. Glazed Pears with Hazelnuts..107

194. Pecan and Carrot Cake..108

195. Cherry Walnut Brownies...108

196. Peanut Butter and Chocolate Balls 109

197. Crispy Sesame Cookies 109

198. Crunchy Almond Cookies 109

199. Frozen Mango Raspberry Delight 110

200. Orange Mug Cake..110

30 Days Meal Plan 111

Measurement Conversion Chart...114

INDEX..115

Conclusion...118

Introduction

What is dash Diet?

DASH (Dietary Approaches to Stop Hypertension) is an eating plan that includes a variety of foods, including fruits, vegetables, whole grains, low-fat dairy products, and lean meats. The diet limits foods and beverages with added sugars and sodium.

The DASH diet focuses on foods that are lower in salt and those rich in important minerals like potassium and calcium, all of which help lower or control blood pressure.

According to WHO (World Health Organization), more than 1 billion people worldwide have high blood pressure — and that number continues to grow. A recent WHO study suggests that the number of adults with high blood pressure has doubled in the last 40 years. This is a serious concern, as high blood pressure is linked to many health problems, including heart disease, kidney failure, and stroke. Diet is believed as a major factor in the development of high blood pressure, so scientific research has taken the lead in studying which diets might benefit people with high blood pressure.

The DASH diet is a heart-healthy eating plan that can help you get your blood pressure under control and it reduce risk of heart disease. Researchers observed that people who followed a plant-based diet, such as vegans and vegetarians, generally had lower blood pressure than others did.

For that reason, the DASH diet, short for Dietary Approaches to Stop Hypertension, focuses its food pyramid on fruits and vegetables while containing lean protein sources like chicken, fish, and beans. It recommends limiting red meats, salt, added sugars, and fat. The reason this diet helps those with high blood pressure is that it reduces salt intake.

The Department of Health in U.S and Human Services recommends that most adults consume no more than 2,300 milligrams (mg) of sodium per day.

Understanding How Dash Diet works

When you start the DASH diet, do not expect to make drastic changes in your eating habits overnight. Instead, start making whatever small changes seem most manageable to you. It is easy to meet your goals if you avoid highly processed foods and eat mostly whole foods instead.

Here are some examples:

- Make sure you eat at least one serving of vegetables or fruit with each meal.
- Add at least two meat-free dishes to your diet each week.
- Experiment with herbs and spices to spice up your recipes and cut down on the amount of salt you use.
- If possible, try using whole-wheat flour instead of white flour in your recipes.
- Instead of reaching for a bag of chips when you are hungry, snack on almonds or pecans. They contain healthy fats that satisfy your appetite better than plain old potato chips.

To achieve the health benefits of DASH, make small changes in your diet each day. By eating a little healthier, you will feel better and lose weight, which will motivate you to continue your healthy eating habits.

Additional Health Benefits

Your diet influences your weight, energy level, and the way you look. There are several ways your diet affects your body. The dash diet focuses mainly on fruits and vegetables. Hence, it has high vitamins and minerals such as folate, calcium, and magnesium, which may be responsible for some of its health benefits. There are other health benefits apart from low blood pressure and weight loss.

1. The DASH diet (Dietary Approaches to Stop Hypertension) might help reduce high blood pressure but offer several other benefits, including reduced risk of cancer and weight loss.

2. Despite what the name suggests, DASH does not necessarily help you lose weight — it was designed to lower blood pressure. Weight loss may simply be a nice side effect of the diet.

3. People who follow the DASH diet have a lower risk of some cancers. Research showed dieters who followed the DASH plan had less risk of colorectal and breast cancer.

4. The DASH diet is scientifically proven to reduce your risk of metabolic syndrome by 81%.

5. The diet has been linked to reducing your risk of type 2 diabetes. Some studies demonstrate that it can improve insulin resistance, making it very effective in preventing type 2 diabetes from developing.

What to eat and what to avoid in DASH diet

Every DASH diet meal plan is unique to you. Therefore, it is hard to give an exact breakdown of a meal plan on a DASH diet for you. The key is to emphasize healthy foods like vegetables and fruits, with less room for salt.

People on a DASH diet plan can eat different amounts of the same foods to stay within target calorie and nutrition limits while keeping the less healthy ones sideline.

To eat in a way that fits the DASH diet, center your meals on foods you like. Try to cook up your favorite meals using less salt or adding more vegetables.

If you do not like green peppers, DASH-friendly alternatives are red peppers, celery, or carrots.

Types of Dash Diets

There are two types of DASH diets: the standard DASH eating plan and a Low sodium DASH diet.

1. The Standard DASH diet suggests people consume no more than 2,300 milligrams of salt per day.

2. The Low Sodium DASH diet has a maximum sodium limit of 1,500 milligrams daily.

People on low-sodium diets need to consume foods with a lot of potassium to counteract the changes in blood pressure caused by the salt restriction. The recommended daily amount is 2,000 mg of potassium (some experts recommend 4,700 mg of Trusted Source of potassium each day).

Potassium is found in variety of delicious foods, including:

- Dried fruit (Apricots, Raisins, etc.)

- Lentils and kidney beans
- Potato
- Orange juice
- Banana

What to Eat

The DASH diet emphasizes the given food categories

- Fresh fruit and vegetables
- Whole grains
- Meat, poultry, and seafood
- Low-fat dairy foods
- Nuts and seeds

Fruits: Fruit is an excellent source of fiber, magnesium, potassium, as well as vitamins and small amounts of other minerals. One serving is a half-cup fresh, canned, or frozen fruit, or one medium fresh fruit.

Vegetables: Vegetables are great, and you can eat any type of vegetable (fiber and vitamin-rich). Examples include broccoli, sweet potatoes, greens, carrots, or tomatoes. A serving could be a half-cup of cooked or raw vegetables.

Whole-grain foods: Such as whole-grain bread, cereals, rice, and pasta. One serving might be a slice of whole-wheat bread, cereals, a half-cup of cooked pasta, rice, or 1 ounce of dry cereal.

Meat, Poultry, and Seafood: Poultry, meat, and seafood are good sources of protein, B vitamins, zinc, and other nutrients. For people following the DASH diet, one serving of meat is 1 oz. cooked, skinless poultry, lean meat, or seafood; 1 egg; or 1 oz. of tuna packed in water.

Low-fat dairy foods: Each of these foods supplies calcium, protein, and vitamins A and D. For one serving, you can have 1 cup of skim milk or fat-free milk, 1.5 ounces of low-fat cheese, or 1 cup of low-fat yogurt.

Nuts and Seeds: Nuts and seeds are good sources of vitamins, minerals, antioxidants, and other nutrients. Here are some examples of healthy snacks: sunflower seeds, beans, peas, lentils, almonds, peanuts, and pistachios.

Compared to other food items, these items have little saturated fat, total fat, and cholesterol.

What to avoid on DASH Diet

Foods to be avoided when following the DASH diet are high-sugar, high-fat snacks, and foods high in salt. A potassium-rich salt substitute can both be used in the kitchen and on the table. It also consists of potassium, which helps lower blood pressure. Individuals on blood pressure medication or those with a high potassium level should consult their doctor about dosage adjustments. Some major food items to be avoided are:

- Candy
- Cookies
- Chips
- Salted nuts
- Sodas
- Sugary beverages
- Pastries
- Snacks
- Meat dishes
- Pizza
- Soups
- Salad dressings
- Cheese
- Cold cuts and cured meats
- Breads and rolls

Shopping List

- Condiments, seasonings, and spreads.
- Lean meats, poultry, and fish.
- Nuts, seeds, and legumes.
- Grains.
- Low-fat dairy products.
- Vegetables
- Fruits

Chapter 1: Breakfasts

1. Vegetarian Breakfast Salad with Eggs

Preparation time: 12 minutes
Cooking time: 5 minutes
Servings: 1
Ingredients:

- 2 Large Free Range Eggs
- 1/8 tsp Black Pepper
- 1 tbsp Lemon Juice
- 1 1/2 tsp olive oil
- 1 1/2 cups Organic Arugula
- 1/8 tsp sea salt
- 1/2 cup avocado
- 3/4 cup Grape Tomatoes
- 1/4 cup Red Onion

Directions:

1. In a serving bowl, whisk together the oil and lemon juice. Add avocado, tomatoes, onion, and arugula, in that sequence, to go on top. Refrigerate overnight with the lid on.
2. Toss the salad to blend in the morning. Add the salt and mix well.
3. Heat an organic cooking spray-coated nonstick skillet over medium heat. Cook for about 4-5 minutes, or until the eggs are sunny-side-up or to your liking.
4. Assemble the salad and top it with the eggs. (Sliced hard-boiled eggs can also be added to the salad.) Add the black pepper and toss to combine.

Per serving: Calories: 58 Kcal; Fat: 40 g; Carbs: 20 g; Protein: 6 g: Sodium: 439 mg; Sugar: 6 g

2. Cheesy Egg in Avocado

Preparation time: 20 minutes
Cooking time: 15 minutes
Servings: 4
Ingredients:

- 1/2 cup shredded cheddar cheese
- Salt and freshly cracked black pepper
- 4 organic eggs
- 2 tbsp olive oil
- 2 medium avocados

Directions:

1. Preheat the oven by turning it on and setting it to 425°F.
2. In the meantime, prepare the avocados by cutting them into two halves and removing their pits.
3. Grease two muffin pans with oil, and fill each with an avocado half.
4. Crack an egg into each half of an avocado, season with salt and freshly cracked black pepper, and top with cheese.
5. Bake the muffin tins for 15 minutes after the oven has preheated.
6. When the avocados baked organic eggs are done, remove them from the muffin tins, place them on a plate, and serve.

Per serving: Calories: 210 Kcal; Fat: 16.6 g; Carbs: 6.4 g; Protein: 10.7 g: Sodium: 151 mg; Sugar: 0.7 g

3. Bulgur Breakfast with Fruits

Preparation time: 10 minutes
Cooking time: 12 minutes
Servings: 12
Ingredients:

- 1 cup chopped almonds
- 1/2 cup fresh mint, chopped
- 4 cups unsweetened almond milk
- 3 cups uncooked bulgur
- 4 cups frozen (or fresh, pitted) dark sweet cherries
- 16 dried (or fresh) figs, chopped
- 2 cups water
- 1 teaspoon ground cinnamon

Directions:

1. In a medium saucepan, whisk together the milk, bulgur, water, and cinnamon.
2. Cover, reduce to medium-low heat, and cook for 10 minutes, or until liquid is absorbed.
3. Remove the pan from the heat but leave it on the burner to whisk in the frozen cherries, figs, and almonds (no need to thaw).
4. Cover and set aside for 1 minute to allow the hot bulgur to partially defrost the cherries and hydrate the figs.
5. Finally, whisk in the mint and serve.

Per serving: Calories: 207 Kcal; Fat: 6 g; Carbs: 32.1 g; Protein: 8 g: Sodium: 82 mg

4. Quinoa Breakfast Bowls

Preparation time: 10 minutes
Cooking time: 10-12 minutes
Servings: 2
Ingredients:
- 1/2 teaspoon salt
- 1 tablespoon chopped fresh dill
- 1/2 cup quinoa, rinsed
- 1 carrot, grated
- 1 small broccoli head, finely chopped
- ¾ cup water, plus additional as needed

Directions:
1. To begin, bring the quinoa and water to a boil in a small pot over high heat.
2. Once the water has boiled, turn the heat down to low. Cover and cook for 5 minutes while stirring occasionally.
3. Add the carrots, broccoli, and salt to the quinoa and cook for another 10 to 12 minutes, or until the quinoa are cooked through and the vegetables are fork-tender.
4. If the mixture becomes too thick, add more water as necessary.
5. Toss in the dill and serve immediately.

Per serving: Calories: 219 Kcal; Fat: 3 g; Carbs: 41 g; Protein: 10 g: Sodium: 619 mg

5. Marinara Poached Eggs

Preparation time: 10 minutes
Cooking time: 10 minutes
Servings: 12
Ingredients:
- 12 large eggs
- 1 cup chopped fresh flat-leaf parsley
- 2 tablespoons extra-virgin olive oil
- 2 cups chopped onion
- 4 (14.5-ounce / 411-g) cans no-salt-added diced tomatoes, undrained
- 4 garlic cloves, minced

Directions:
1. In a large skillet, heat the olive oil over medium-high heat.
2. Add the onion and cook, stirring periodically, for 5 minutes.
3. Cook for a further minute after adding the garlic.
4. Finally, pour the tomatoes and their juices over the onion mixture and cook for 2 to 3 minutes, or until the mixture is boiling.
5. Reduce the heat to medium and form six indentations in the tomato mixture with a big spoon.
6. Crack the eggs into each indentation one at a time.
7. Cover and simmer for 6 to 7 minutes, or until the eggs are cooked to your liking.
8. Finish with a sprinkling of parsley on top.

Per serving: Calories: 89 Kcal; Fat: 6 g; Carbs: 4 g; Protein: 4 g: Sodium: 77 mg

6. Low Carb Green Smoothie

Preparation time: 15 minutes
Cooking time: 0 minutes
Servings: 4
Ingredients:

- ½ cup kiwi fruit, peeled and chopped
- 1 tablespoon Swerve
- 3 cups filtered water
- 1/8 cup fresh pineapple, chopped
- ¾ tablespoon fresh parsley
- 1 cup romaine lettuce
- 1tablespoon fresh ginger, peeled and chopped
- 1 cup raw cucumber, peeled and sliced
- 1/2 Hass avocado

Directions:

1. Take a blender, combine all of the ingredients, and puree until smooth.
2. Strain into two serving glasses and chill until ready to serve.

Per serving: Calories: 110 Kcal; Fat: 9 g; Carbs: 8 g; Protein: 1.5 g: Sodium: 24 mg

7. Fig with Ricotta Oatmeal

Preparation time: 5 minutes

Cooking time: 8-10 minutes

Servings: 2

Ingredients:

- 2 tablespoons almonds, toasted, sliced
- 4 tablespoons dried figs, chopped
- 2 cups water
- Pinch of salt
- 4 teaspoons honey
- 4 tablespoons ricotta cheese, part-skim
- 1 cup old-fashioned rolled oats

Directions:

1. Bring the water to a boil in a small saucepan with the salt.
2. Next, add the oats and turn the heat down to medium. Cook the oats for about 5 minutes, until most of the water has been absorbed, stirring regularly.
3. Turn off the heat, cover the pan, and set aside for 2-3 minutes.
4. Toss with figs, almonds, ricotta, and honey drizzle before serving.

Per serving: Calories: 316 Kcal; Fat: g; 8 Carbs: 10 g; Protein: 10 g: Sodium: 360 mg

8. Grilled Basil Lemon Tofu Burgers

Preparation time: 5 minutes

Cooking time: 10 minutes

Servings: 12

Ingredients:

- 4 tablespoons honey
- 1/2 cup freshly squeezed lemon juice
- 2 garlic cloves, minced
- 1 cup Kalamata olives, finely, chopped pitted
- 6 tablespoons sour cream, reduced-fat
- 2 cups watercress, trimmed
- 4 teaspoons grated lemon rind
- 12 slices (1/4-inch thick each) tomato
- 12 pieces (1 1/2-ounce) whole-wheat hamburger buns
- 4 tablespoons Dijon mustard
- 2 tablespoons olive oil, extra-virgin,
- 6 tablespoons light mayonnaise
- 2 pounds tofu, firm or extra-firm, drained
- 1 teaspoon salt
- 1/2 teaspoon black pepper (freshly ground)
- 6 garlic cloves, minced
- Cooking spray
- 1 cup fresh basil, finely chopped

Directions:

1. In a small dish, whisk together all of the marinade ingredients.
2. Slice the tofu into 6 in a transverse direction.
3. Using paper towels, pat each slice dry.
4. Next, arrange the slices on a jelly roll pan and coat both sides with the marinade mixture; set aside any excess marinade. 1 hour to marinate
5. Coat the grill rack with cooking spray and preheat the grill.

6. Arrange the tofu slices on the grill and cook for 3 minutes per side, coating the tofu with the marinade mixture that was set aside.

7. Mix the garlic-olive mayonnaise ingredients together in a small bowl.

8. Spread about 1 1/2 tablespoons of the mixture on the bottom half of each hamburger bun.

9. Finally, top each with a slice of tofu, a slice of tomato, and roughly 2 tablespoons of watercress before adding the top buns.

Per serving: Calories: 275 Kcal; Fat: 11 g; Carbs: 35 g; Protein: 10.5 g: Sodium: 740 mg

9. Smoked Salmon Avocado Toast

Preparation time: 10 minutes

Cooking time: 3 minutes

Servings: 1

Ingredients:

- 1/2 medium avocado
- 3 oz. smoked salmon
- 1 pinch perfect pinch salt free garlic & herb seasoning
- 2 slice sprouted whole grain bread

Directions:

1. Preheat the oven to 350°F. Toast the two slices of bread and spread the avocado evenly between them.

2. Spread the spices on the avocado, and then top with the wild salmon.

3. Put the other slice over it and serve immediately.

Per serving: Calories: 21 Kcal; Fat: 3 g; Carbs: 7 g; Protein: 24 g: Sodium: 889 mg

10. Delicious Fluffy Almond Flour Pancakes

Preparation time: 12 minutes

Cooking time: 10 minutes

Servings: 12

Ingredients:

- 1/2 greek yogurt
- 2 Cup diced strawberries
- 2 Cups almond flour
- 2 Tbsp maple syrup
- 2 Tsp baking powder
- 4 Eggs

Optional icing:

- 1 Cup powdered sugar
- Mediavine
- 2 Tbsp milk
- 1 Tsp vanilla

Directions:

1. Whisk your almond flour and baking powder together in a mixing basin.

2. Next, whisk together the eggs, maple syrup, and Greek yoghurt until a thick batter is formed.

3. Add the diced strawberries and stir to combine.

4. Heat a frying pan over medium to low heat, sprayed with nonstick olive oil spray or a little amount of butter.

5. Scoop the batter into the pan with a 1/4-cup measuring cup.

6. Cover with the lid and simmer for 2-3 minutes on low heat.

7. When ready to flip, cook for about a minute on the other side before removing from the fire and placing on a plate.

8. For a sweeter treat, top with extra strawberries, coconut whipped cream, maple syrup, or our optional frosting.

Per serving: Calories: 193 Kcal; Fat: 11 g; Carbs: 18 g; Protein: g: 7 Sodium: 110 mg

11. Mediterranean Breakfast Eggs

Preparation time: 15 minutes

Cooking time: 10 minutes

Servings: 8

Ingredients:
- 1/2 Teaspoon turmeric
- 8 Large eggs
- 1/2 Cup chopped fresh cilantro
- 2 (14.5-ounce/ 411-g) can diced tomatoes, drained
- 1/2 Teaspoon ground cardamom
- 1/2 Teaspoon paprika
- 4 Tablespoons extra-virgin olive oil
- 2 Cups finely diced potato
- 2 Cups chopped red bell peppers
- 2 Cups chopped shallots
- 2 Teaspoons garlic powder

Directions:
1. First, preheat the oven to 350 degrees Fahrenheit (180 degrees Celsius).
2. Then, in an ovenproof skillet, heat the olive oil until it simmers over medium-high heat.
3. Add the shallots and cook for 3 minutes, or until aromatic, stirring regularly.
4. Stir to mix the garlic powder, potato, and bell peppers.
5. Cook, stirring often, for 10 minutes, covered.
6. In a large mixing bowl, combine the tomatoes, cardamom, paprika, and turmeric.
7. Remove the skillet from the heat when the mixture starts to bubble, and crack the eggs into it.
8. Bake for 5 to 10 minutes, or until the egg whites are set and the yolks are cooked to your preference, in a preheated oven.
9. Remove the dish from the oven and top with cilantro before serving.

Per serving: Calories: 225 Kcal; Fat: 12 g; Carbs: 20 g; Protein: 9 g: Sodium: 278 mg

12. Morning Overnight Oats with Raspberries

Preparation time: 5 minutes
Cooking time: 0 minutes
Servings: 4
Ingredients:
- 1/4 Teaspoon ground cinnamon
- Pinch ground cloves
- 1.1/2 Cup unsweetened almond milk
- 1/2 Cup raspberries
- 2 Teaspoon honey
- 1/2 Teaspoon turmeric
- 2/3 Cup rolled oats

Directions:
1. To begin, fill a mason jar halfway with almond milk, raspberries, rolled oats, honey, turmeric, cinnamon, and cloves.
2. To combine the ingredients, cover and shake well.
3. Refrigerate for at least eight hours, preferably twenty-four hours.
4. Chill and serve.

Per serving: Calories: 81 Kcal; Fat: g; 1.9 Carbs: 14 g; Protein: 2.1 g: Sodium: 97 mg

13. Morning Mediterranean Frittata

Preparation time: 15 minutes
Cooking time: 15 minutes
Servings: 6
Ingredients:
- 1/4 cup olive oil
- 1 sweet red pepper, diced
- 1 medium zucchini, cut to 1/2-inch cubes
- 1/2 cup onion, chopped
- 9 large eggs, lightly beaten
- 1 package (4 ounce) feta cheese, crumbled

- 1/3 cup parmesan cheese, freshly grated
- 1/3 cup fresh basil, thinly sliced
- 1/2 teaspoon salt
- 1/2 teaspoon pepper
- 8 Kalamata olives, pitted, chopped

Directions:

1. Heat the olive oil in a 10-inch oven-safe skillet until very hot.
2. Cook, stirring regularly, until the olives, zucchini, red pepper, and onions are soft.
3. In a mixing bowl, whisk together the eggs, feta cheese, basil, salt, and pepper; pour into the vegetable-filled skillet.
4. Reduce to a low heat, cover, and cook for 10-12 minutes, or until the egg mixture is almost set.
5. Finally, take the pan from the heat and top with parmesan cheese. Place the broiler on top of the meat.
6. Broil for about 2-3 minutes, or until the top is brown, with the oven door half-ajar.
7. Make wedges out of them.

Per serving: Calories: 288.5 Kcal; Fat: g; 23 Carbs: 5.6 g; Protein: 15.1 g: Sodium: 559 mg

14. Dried Cranberries Cinnamon Oatmeal

Preparation time: 10 minutes
Cooking time: 5-8 minutes
Servings: 4
Ingredients:

- 2 cups water
- Pinch sea salt
- 2 cups old-fashioned oats
- 2 cups almond milk
- 1 cup dried cranberries
- 2 teaspoons ground cinnamon

Directions:

1. Bring the almond milk, water, and salt to a boil over high heat in a medium saucepan.
2. Then add the oats, cranberries, and cinnamon and whisk to combine. Cook, stirring periodically, for 5 minutes over medium heat.
3. Turn off the heat under the oatmeal. Allow for 3 minutes of rest time after covering. Before serving, give the mixture another stir.

Per serving: Calories: 108 Kcal; Fat: g; 2.1 Carbs: 18.4 g; Protein: 3.3 g: Sodium: 123 mg

15. Corn Banana Fritters

Preparation time: 20 minutes
Cooking time: 5 minutes
Servings: 4
Ingredients:

- 1 teaspoon baking powder
- 1 teaspoon ground chipotle chili
- 2 tablespoons olive oil
- 1 cup yellow cornmeal
- 1/2 cup flour
- 1/2 teaspoon ground cinnamon
- 1/2 teaspoon sea salt
- 4 small ripe bananas, peeled and mashed
- 4 tablespoons unsweetened almond milk
- 2 large eggs, beaten

Directions:

1. In a large mixing basin, whisk together all ingredients except the olive oil until smooth.
2. Then, over medium-high heat, heat a nonstick skillet.
3. Finally, drizzle in the olive oil and drop around 2 tablespoons of batter per fritter.
4. Cook for 2 to 3 minutes, or until golden brown on the bottoms, then flip.

5. Cook for another 1 to 2 minutes, or until well cooked.

6. Continue with the rest of the batter.

Per serving: Calories: 400 Kcal; Fat: 10.5 g; Carbs: 68 g; Protein: 7.3 g: Sodium: 307 mg

16. Healthy Avocado Smoothie

Preparation time: 5 minutes

Cooking time: 0 minutes

Servings: 4

Ingredients:

- 3 cups unsweetened coconut milk
- 4 tablespoons honey
- 2 large avocados

Directions:

1. Take a blender, combine all of the ingredients, and blend until smooth and creamy.

Per serving: Calories: 690 Kcal; Fat: 57.6 g; Carbs: 39 g; Protein: 6 g: Sodium: 35 mg

17. Simple Apple Tahini Toast

Preparation time: 10 minutes

Cooking time: 3 minutes

Servings: 2

Ingredients:

- 4 slices whole-wheat bread, toasted
- 4 tablespoons tahini
- 2 teaspoons honey
- 2 small apples of your choice, thinly sliced

Directions:

1. On the toasted bread, spread the tahini.
2. Spread the slices of apples on toast.
3. Drizzle honey over the apple slices and serve.

Per serving: Calories: 460 Kcal; Fat: 18 g; Carbs: g; 63 Protein: 11 g: Sodium: 280 mg

18. Savory Breakfast Oatmeal

Preparation time: 10 minutes

Cooking time: 15 minutes

Servings: 4

Ingredients:

- Sea salt and freshly ground pepper, to taste
- 2 cups water
- 2 large tomatoes, chopped
- 2 tablespoons olive oil
- 1 cup steel-cut oats
- 2 medium cucumbers, chopped
- Pinch freshly grated Parmesan cheese
- Flat-leaf parsley or mint, chopped, for garnishing

Directions:

1. In a medium saucepan, combine the oats and water and bring to a boil over high heat, stirring constantly, for 15 minutes, or until the water is absorbed.

2. Finally, split the oats between two dishes and top with the tomato and cucumber. Drizzle the olive oil over the top and top with the Parmesan cheese.

3. Season to taste with salt and pepper.

4. Garnish with parsley before serving.

Per serving: Calories: 200 Kcal; Fat: 9 g; Carbs: 23 g; Protein: 6.4 g: Sodium: 25 mg

19. Baked Avocado Eggs

Preparation time: 12-15 minutes

Cooking time: 15 minutes

Servings: 4

Ingredients:

- Kosher salt and black pepper, to taste
- 4 eggs
- 2 medium sized avocados, halved and pit removed
- 1/2 cup cheddar cheese, shredded

Directions:

1. Preheat the oven to 425°F and lightly butter a muffin tray.
2. Crack an egg into each avocado half and season with salt and black pepper.
3. Remove the muffin tray from the oven. Place the avocado in the tray and cover with cheddar cheese.
4. Remove from the oven and set aside to cool for about 15 minutes before serving.

Per serving: Calories: 210 Kcal; Fat: g; 16.5 Carbs: 6.5 g; Protein: 10.5 g: Sodium: 2.3 mg

20. Easy Berry and Nut Parfait

Preparation time: 10 minutes
Cooking time: 0 minutes
Servings: 4

Ingredients:
- 2 Cup fresh blueberries
- 1 Cup walnut pieces
- 4 Cups plain Greek yogurt
- 2 Cup fresh raspberries
- 4 Tablespoons honey

Directions:
1. In a medium mixing basin, whisk together the yoghurt and honey. Divide the mixture between two serving dishes.
2. Finally, sprinkle 2 cup blueberries, 2 cup raspberries, and 4 cup walnut bits on top of each. Serve right away.

Per serving: Calories: 505 Kcal; Fat: g; 23 Carbs: 57 g; Protein: 24 g: Sodium: 172 mg

Chapter 2: Salads and Sides

21. Rainbow Slaw

Preparation time: 10 minutes
Cooking time: 0 minutes
Servings: 6
Ingredients:

- 2 tsp honey
- 1 tbsp rice vinegar
- 1 cup cherry tomatoes halved
- 1 medium yellow bell pepper diced
- 1/4 cup chopped fresh parsley
- 2 tbsp mayonnaise
- 2 tbsp nonfat, plain Greek yogurt
- 3/4 tsp celery salt
- 14 oz. coleslaw mix

Directions:

1. Mayonnaise, yoghurt, honey, rice vinegar, and celery salt are whisked together in a medium bowl. Mix everything up thoroughly.
2. Combine the coleslaw, tomatoes, pepper, onion, and parsley in a large mixing bowl. Toss gently until all of the dressing is distributed evenly.
3. Serve immediately or preserve for up to 3 days in the refrigerator.

Per serving: Calories: 78 Kcal; Fat: 4 g; Carbs: 10 g; Protein: 2 g: Sodium: 205 mg

22. Dash Diet Waldorf Salad

Preparation time: 15 minutes
Cooking time: 0 minutes
Servings: 4
Ingredients:

- 2 tbsp whole-egg mayonnaise
- 2 tbsp lemon juice
- 2 medium red delicious apples
- 1/2 cup walnuts
- 1/4 small red onion, thinly sliced
- 3 celery stalks, leaves reserved

Directions:

1. In a large mixing bowl, pour half of the lemon juice. Apples should be halved and cored. Slice thinly. Mix the apple with the lemon juice (see note). Toss gently to coat.
2. In a mixing bowl, combine mayonnaise and the remaining lemon juice. Add Salt & pepper to taste. Prepare the celery by slicing the stalks thinly and chopping the leaves.
3. Toss the apple mixture with the celery, celery leaves, walnuts, and onion. Toss gently to blend. Drizzle with the mayonnaise mixture before serving.

Per serving: Calories: 213 Kcal; Fat: 17 g; Carbs: 14 g; Protein: 3 g: Sodium: 88 mg

23. Shrimp & Nectarine Salad

Preparation time: 15 minutes
Cooking time: 7 minutes
Servings: 4
Ingredients:

- 1-1/2 teaspoons honey
- 1 tablespoon minced fresh tarragon
- 1/3 cup orange juice
- 1-1/2 teaspoons Dijon mustard
- 3 tablespoons cider vinegar

Salad:

- 4 teaspoons canola oil, divided
- 1 cup fresh or frozen corn
- 1 pound uncooked shrimp (26-30 per pound), peeled and deveined
- 1/2 teaspoon lemon-pepper seasoning
- 1/4 teaspoon salt
- 8 cups torn mixed salad greens
- 2 medium nectarines, cut into 1-inch pieces

- 1 cup grape tomatoes, halved
- 1/2 cup finely chopped red onion

Directions:

1. Whisk orange juice, vinegar, mustard, and honey together in a small bowl until well combined.
2. Add the tarragon and mix well.
3. 1 teaspoon oil, heated in a large skillet over medium-high heat. Cook and stir for 1-2 minutes, or until corn is crisp-tender.
4. Remove the pan from the heat.
5. Season the shrimp with salt and lemon pepper. Heat the remaining oil in the same skillet over medium-high heat.
6. Cook and stir for 3-4 minutes, or until shrimp are pink.
7. Add the corn and mix well.
8. Combine the remaining ingredients in a large mixing bowl. Drizzle 1/3 cup dressing over the salad and toss to coat.
9. Using four plates, divide the mixture. Drizzle the remaining dressing over the shrimp mixture. Serve right away.

Per serving: Calories: 252 Kcal; Fat: 138 g; Carbs: 27 g; Protein: 23 g: Sodium: 442 mg

24. Roasted Sweet Potato & Chickpea Pitas

Preparation time: 10 minutes

Cooking time: 20 minutes

Servings: 6

Ingredients:

- 1 teaspoon ground cumin
- 2 cups arugula or baby spinach
- 12 whole wheat pita pocket halves, warmed
- 2 medium sweet potatoes (about 1-1/4 pounds), peeled and cubed
- 3 tablespoons canola oil, divided
- 2 teaspoons garam masala
- 1 tablespoon lemon juice
- 2 cans (15 ounces each) chickpeas or garbanzo beans, rinsed and drained
- 1 medium red onion, chopped

- 1/4 cup minced fresh cilantro
- 1/2 teaspoon salt, divided
- 2 garlic cloves, minced
- 1 cup plain Greek yogurt

Directions:

1. Preheat the oven to 400 degrees Fahrenheit. Microwave potatoes for 5 minutes on high, covered, in a large microwave-safe bowl.
2. Toss with 2 tablespoons oil, garam masala, and 1/4 teaspoon salt after adding chickpeas and onion.
3. Fill a 15x10x1-inch baking pan halfway with batter. Roast for 15 minutes, or until potatoes are soft. Allow to cool slightly.
4. In a small microwave-safe bowl, combine garlic and remaining oil; microwave on high for 1 to 1-1/2 minutes, or until garlic is gently browned.
5. Combine the yoghurt, lemon juice, cumin, and the remaining salt in a mixing bowl.
6. Toss the arugula with the potato mixture. Fill pitas halfway with the filling, and then top with the sauce and cilantro.

Per serving: Calories: 462 Kcal; Fat: 1 g; Carbs: 10 mg; Protein: 14 g: Sodium: 660

25. Strawberry-Blue Cheese Steak Salad

Preparation time: 20 minutes

Cooking time: 5-7 minutes

Servings: 4

Ingredients:

- 2 teaspoons olive oil
- 2 tablespoons lime juice
- 1 beef top sirloin steak (3/4 inch thick and 1 pound)
- 1/2 teaspoon salt
- 1/4 teaspoon pepper

Salad:

- 2 cups fresh strawberries, halved
- 1 bunch romaine, torn
- 1/4 cup chopped walnuts, toasted
- Reduced-fat balsamic vinaigrette
- 1/4 cup thinly sliced red onion
- 1/4 cup crumbled blue cheese

Directions:

1. Season the meat with salt and pepper before serving.
2. Heat the oil in a large skillet over medium heat.
3. Cook 5-7 minutes on each side until steak reaches desired doneness (a thermometer should register 135° for medium-rare, 140° for medium, and 145° for medium-well).
4. Remove from the pan and set aside for 5 minutes. Toss steak with lime juice and cut into bite-size strips.
5. Combine romaine, strawberries, and onion on a dish; top with steak. Cheese and walnuts should be sprinkled on top.
6. Toss with vinaigrette before serving.

Per serving: Calories: 290 Kcal; Fat: 15 g; Carbs: 12 g; Protein: 29 g: Sodium: 450

26. Turkey Medallions with Tomato Salad

Preparation time: 15 minutes

Cooking time: 30 minutes

Servings: 6

Ingredients:

- 1 tablespoon thinly sliced fresh basil
- 3 medium-sized tomatoes
- 2 tablespoons olive oil
- 1 tablespoon red wine vinegar
- 1/2 teaspoon sugar
- 1 celery rib, coarsely chopped
- 1/4 cup chopped red onion
- 1/4 teaspoon dried oregano
- 1/4 teaspoon salt
- 1 medium green pepper, coarsely chopped

Turkey:

- 1/4 teaspoon pepper
- 1 package (20 ounces) turkey breast tenderloins
- 1/4 teaspoon salt
- 3 tablespoons olive oil
- Fresh basil
- 1/2 cup grated Parmesan cheese
- 1 large egg
- 2 tablespoons lemon juice
- 1 cup panko bread crumbs
- 1 teaspoon lemon-pepper seasoning
- 1/2 cup finely chopped walnuts

Directions:

1. Combine the first five ingredients in a mixing bowl. Green pepper, celery, onion, and basil should all be added at this point. Cut tomatoes into wedges and half the wedges.
2. Add to the pepper mixture and combine well.
3. Whisk the egg and lemon juice together in a small bowl.
4. Toss in the bread crumbs with cheese, walnuts, and lemon pepper in a separate shallow bowl.
5. Tenderloins should be cut crosswise into 1-inch slices and flattened with a meat mallet to a 1/2-inch thickness. Season to taste with salt and pepper.
6. Dip in the egg mixture, and then pat in the crumb mixture to adhere.
7. Heat 1 tablespoon oil in a large skillet over medium-high heat Cook until a third of the turkey is golden brown, about 2-3 minutes per side.
8. Repeat with the remaining oil and turkey twice more. Serve with the tomato mixture and basil on top.

Per serving: Calories: 251 Kcal; Fat: 21 g; Carbs: 13 g; Protein: 30 g: Sodium: 452 mg

27. Warm Rice and Pinto Salad

Preparation time: 15 minutes

Cooking time: 15 minutes

Servings: 4

Ingredients:

- 1/4 cup chopped fresh cilantro
- 1 bunch romaine, quartered lengthwise through the core
- 1/4 cup finely shredded low fat cheese
- 1 tablespoon olive oil
- 1 cup frozen corn
- 1-1/2 teaspoons ground cumin
- 1 can (15 ounces) pinto beans, rinsed and drained
- 1 can (4 ounces) chopped green chiles
- 1 small onion, chopped
- 2 garlic cloves, minced
- 1-1/2 teaspoons chili powder
- 1/2 cup salsa
- 1 package (8.8 ounces) ready-to-serve brown rice

Directions:

1. Heat the oil in a large skillet over medium-high heat. Cook and stir the corn and onion for 4-5 minutes or until onion is soft.
2. Cook and stir for another minute after adding the garlic, chili powder, and cumin.
3. Heat through, stirring occasionally, the beans, rice, green chiles, salsa, and cilantro.
4. Serve with romaine wedges on the side. Cheese should be sprinkled on top.

Per serving: Calories: 330 Kcal; Fat: 6 g; Carbs: 46 g; Protein: 12 g: Sodium: 462 mg

28. Grilled Southwestern Steak Salad

Preparation time: 20 minutes

Cooking time: 25 minutes

Servings: 4

Ingredients:

- 1 tablespoon olive oil
- 2 cups uncooked multigrain bow tie pasta
- 1 beef top sirloin steak (almost 1 inch thick and 3/4 pound)
- 1/4 teaspoon salt
- 2 large ears sweet corn, husks removed
- 1 large sized sweet onion, cut into 1/2-inch rings
- 2 large tomatoes
- 1/4 teaspoon ground cumin
- 1/4 teaspoon pepper
- 3 poblano peppers, halved and seeded

Dressing:

- 1/4 teaspoon pepper
- 1/3 cup chopped fresh cilantro
- 1/4 cup lime juice
- 1/4 teaspoon salt
- 1/4 teaspoon ground cumin
- 1 tablespoon olive oil

Directions:

1. Rub salt, cumin, and pepper into the steak.
2. Apply oil to the poblano peppers, corn, and onion. Cook 7-9 minutes on each side, or until meat is cooked as desired. (a thermometer should register 135° for medium-rare, 140° for medium, and 145° for medium-well).
3. Cover and grill for 8-10 minutes, or until crisp-tender, flipping once or twice.
4. Follow the package guidelines for cooking pasta.
5. Meanwhile, remove the corn from the cob and coarsely chop the peppers, onion, and tomatoes.
6. Fill a large mixing bowl halfway with veggies. Mix lime juice, oil, salt, cumin, and pepper in a small bowl until well combined; add cilantro and toss to combine.
7. Drain the pasta and combine it with the vegetables in a large mixing bowl. Toss to coat with the dressing.
8. Thinly slice the steak and serve with the salad.

Per serving: Calories: 458 Kcal; Fat: 13 g; Carbs: 58 g; Protein: 31 g: Sodium: 375 mg

29. Thai-Style Cobb Salad

Preparation time: 15 minutes

Cooking time: 0 minutes

Servings: 6

Ingredients:

- 3/4 cup Asian toasted sesame salad dressing
- 1 cup fresh snow peas, halved
- 1/2 cup unsalted peanuts
- 1/4 cup fresh cilantro leaves
- 1 medium avocado, peeled, ripe and thinly sliced
- 1 medium carrot, shredded
- 2 tablespoons creamy peanut butter
- 1 bunch romaine, torn
- 2 cups shredded rotisserie chicken
- 3 hard-boiled large eggs, coarsely chopped
- 1 medium sweet red pepper, julienned

Directions:

1. On a large serving dish, arrange the romaine. Sprinkle cilantro over romaine and top with chicken, eggs, avocado, veggies, and peanuts.
2. Take a small bowl and whisk together salad dressing and peanut butter until smooth.
3. Serve it with salad and enjoy.

Per serving: Calories: 384 Kcal; Fat: 25 g; Carbs: 18 g; Protein: 23 g: Sodium: 462 mg

30. Cherry-Chicken Lettuce Wraps

Preparation time: 20 minutes

Cooking time: 5 minutes

Servings: 4

Ingredients:

- 2 tablespoons reduced-sodium teriyaki sauce
- 1 tablespoon honey
- 8 Bibb or Boston lettuce leaves
- 1-1/2 cups shredded carrots
- 1-1/4 cups coarsely chopped pitted fresh sweet cherries
- 4 green onions, chopped
- 3/4 pound skinless, boneless chicken breasts, cut into 3/4-inch cubes
- 1 teaspoon ground ginger
- 1/4 teaspoon salt
- 1/4 teaspoon pepper
- 2 teaspoons olive oil
- 1/3 cup coarsely chopped almonds
- 2 tablespoons rice vinegar

Directions:

1. Ginger, salt, and pepper should be sprinkled over the chicken. Heat the oil in a large nonstick skillet over medium-high heat.
2. Cook and stir for 3-5 minutes, or until the chicken is no longer pink.
3. Remove the pan from the heat. Combine carrots, cherries, green onions, and almonds in a mixing bowl.
4. Combine vinegar, teriyaki sauce, and honey in a small basin; stir into chicken mixture.
5. Fill lettuce leaves halfway with filling; fold lettuce over filling.

Per serving: Calories: 256 Kcal; Fat: 10 g; Carbs: 22 g; Protein: 21 g: Sodium: 380 mg

31. Lentil Medley

Preparation time: 15 minutes

Cooking time: 25 minutes

Servings: 8

Ingredients:

- 1 teaspoon dried oregano
- 4 cups fresh baby spinach, chopped
- 1 cup (4 ounces) crumbled feta cheese
- 1 small red onion, chopped
- 1/2 cup chopped soft sun-dried tomato halves (not packed in oil)
- 1/2 cup rice vinegar
- 4 bacon strips, cooked and crumbled, optional

- 1 cup dried lentils, rinsed
- 2 cups water
- 1/4 cup minced fresh mint
- 3 tablespoons olive oil
- 2 cups sliced fresh mushrooms
- 1 medium cucumber, cubed
- 1 medium zucchini, cubed
- 2 teaspoons honey
- 1 teaspoon dried basil

Directions:

1. In a small pot, place the lentils and some water. Bring the water to a boil. Reduce heat to low and cook, covered, for 20-25 minutes or until vegetables are soft. Rinse in cold water after draining.
2. Place in a large mixing basin.
3. Mushrooms, cucumber, zucchini, onion, and tomatoes are all good additions.
4. Whisk together the vinegar, mint, oil, honey, basil, and oregano in a small basin.
5. Drizzle over the lentils and toss to coat. Toss in the spinach, cheese, and, if preferred, bacon.

Per serving: Calories: 225 Kcal; Fat: 8.1 g; Carbs: 28 g; Protein: 10 g: Sodium: 400 mg

32. Spicy Almonds

Preparation time: 10 minutes

Cooking time: 30 minutes

Servings: 8-10 (Total 2.5 cups)

Ingredients:

- 1/2 teaspoon ground cumin
- 1 large egg white, room temperature
- 2-1/2 cups unblanched almonds
- 1 teaspoon paprika
- 1 tablespoon sugar
- 1-1/2 teaspoons kosher salt
- 1/2 teaspoon ground cinnamon
- 1/2 teaspoon ground coriander
- 1/4 teaspoon cayenne pepper

Directions:

1. Preheat the oven to 325 degrees Fahrenheit.
2. Combine the first 7 ingredients in a small bowl. In a separate small dish, whisk the egg white until it becomes frothy.
3. Toss in the almonds to coat. Toss with the spice mixture to coat. In a greased 15x10x1-inch baking pan, spread in a single layer.
4. Preheat oven to 350°F and bake for 30 minutes, stirring every 10 minutes.
5. Allow to cool completely on waxed paper. Keep in a sealed container.

Per serving: Calories: 230 Kcal; Fat: 20 g; Carbs: 9 g; Protein: 8 g: Sodium: 292 mg

33. Italian Sausage-Stuffed Zucchini

Preparation time: 35 minutes

Cooking time: 20 minutes

Servings: 6

Ingredients:

- 1/4 teaspoon pepper
- 3/4 cup shredded part-skim mozzarella cheese
- Additional minced fresh parsley, optional
- 6 medium zucchini (about 8 ounces each)
- 1 pound Italian turkey sausage links, casings removed
- 2 medium tomatoes, seeded and chopped
- 1/3 cup minced fresh parsley
- 2 tablespoons minced fresh oregano
- 2 tablespoons minced fresh basil
- 1 cup panko bread crumbs
- 1/3 cup grated Parmesan cheese

Directions:

1. Preheat the oven to 350 degrees. Cut each zucchini in half lengthwise. Scoop out the pulp, leaving a quarter-inch shell; chop the pulp.

2. Fill a large microwave-safe dish halfway with zucchini shells.
3. Microwave on high for 2-3 minutes, covered, in batches until crisp-tender.
4. Cook sausage and zucchini pulp in a large skillet over medium heat for 6-8 minutes, or until sausage is no longer pink, breaking it up into crumbs; drain.
5. Combine tomatoes, bread crumbs, Parmesan cheese, herbs, and pepper in a mixing bowl.
6. Fill zucchini shells with the filling.
7. Place in two 13x9-inch baking dishes that have not been oiled.
8. Cover and bake for 15-20 minutes, until zucchini is soft.
9. Lastly, top with mozzarella cheese. Bake for another 5-8 minutes, uncovered, or until cheese is melted. Add more minced parsley if desired.

Per serving: Calories: 205 Kcal; Fat: 9 g; Carbs: 16 g; Protein: 17 g: Sodium: 472 mg

34. Chickpea Mint Tabbouleh

Preparation time: 20 minutes
Cooking time: 5-10 minutes
Servings: 4
Ingredients:

- 2 tablespoons soft sun-dried tomatoes (not packed in oil)
- 1 can chickpeas beans, rinsed and drained (almost 15 ounces)
- 1/2 teaspoon salt
- 1 cup bulgur
- 1/2 cup minced fresh parsley
- 1/4 cup minced fresh mint
- 1/4 cup olive oil
- 2 cups water
- 1 cup peas (about 5 ounces), thawed (fresh or frozen)
- 2 tablespoons lemon juice
- 1/4 teaspoon pepper

Directions:

1. Bring bulgur and water to a boil in a big pot. Reduce to a low heat and cook for 10 minutes, covered.
2. Cook, covered, for 5 minutes until bulgur and peas are soft.
3. In a large mixing basin, combine all of the ingredients.
4. Add the rest of the ingredients and mix thoroughly. Serve hot or cold, depending on your preference.

Per serving: Calories: 279 Kcal; Fat: 16 g; Carbs: 51 g; Protein: 11 g: Sodium: 448 mg

35. Pesto Corn Salad with Shrimp

Preparation time: 20 minutes
Cooking time: 10-15 minutes
Servings: 4
Ingredients:

- 1 medium ripe avocado, peeled and chopped
- 1 pound uncooked shrimp (31-40 per pound), peeled and deveined
- 4 medium ears sweet corn, husked
- 1/2 cup packed fresh basil leaves
- 1-1/2 cups cherry tomatoes, halved
- 1/8 teaspoon pepper
- 1/4 cup olive oil
- 1/2 teaspoon salt, divided

Directions:

1. Cook corn until soft in a pot of boiling water, about 5 minutes.
2. Drain and set aside to cool slightly. Meanwhile, pulse basil, oil, and 1/4 teaspoon salt in a food processor until smooth.
3. Remove the corn from the cob and place it in a basin.
4. Add the tomatoes, pepper, and the remaining salt and stir to combine.
5. Toss in the avocado and 2 tablespoons of the basil mixture gently to incorporate.

6. Brush the remaining basil mixture over the shrimp on metal or moistened wooden skewers.
7. Cover and grill over medium heat for 2-4 minutes per side, or until shrimp turn pink.
8. Remove the shrimp from the skewers and combine with the corn mixture.
9. Serve immediately and enjoy.

Per serving: Calories: 150 Kcal; Fat: 2 g; Carbs: 1g; Protein: 8g: Sodium: 150mg

36. Southwest Shredded Pork Salad

Preparation time: 20 minutes

Cooking time: 6 hours (in a slow cooker)

Servings: 12

Ingredients:

- 1 can (15 ounces) black beans, rinsed and drained
- 2 medium tomatoes, chopped
- 1 small red onion, chopped
- 1 cup fresh or frozen corn
- 1 boneless pork loin roast (almost 3-4 pounds)
- 12 cups torn mixed salad greens
- 1 cup shredded part-skim mozzarella cheese
- Salad dressing of your choice
- 1 can (4 ounces) chopped green chiles, drained
- 1 teaspoon chili powder
- 1 teaspoon pepper
- 1/2 teaspoon ground cumin
- 1-1/2 cups apple cider or juice
- 1/2 teaspoon dried oregano
- 3 garlic cloves, minced
- 1-1/2 teaspoons salt
- 1-1/2 teaspoons hot pepper sauce

Directions:

1. Place the meat in a 5-6 quart slow cooker.
2. Mix the cider, green chiles, garlic, salt, pepper sauce, chili powder, pepper, cumin, and oregano together in a small dish; pour over the pork.
3. Cook for 6-8 hours on low flame, covered, until the meat is cooked.
4. Cooking juices should be discarded after removing the roast from the slow cooker. Use 2 forks for shredding pork and prepare a big serving plate with salad greens.
5. Add pork, black beans, tomatoes, onion, corn, and cheese to the top. You can serve with salad dressing.

Per serving: Calories: 233 Kcal; Fat: 8 g; Carbs: 12 g; Protein: 28 g: Sodium: 321 mg

37. Edamame Salad with Sesame Ginger Dressing

Preparation time: 15 minutes

Cooking time: 0 minutes

Servings: 6

Ingredients:

- 1/2 cup salted peanuts
- 1 can garbanzo beans or chickpeas, rinsed and drained (15 ounces)
- 2 green onions, diagonally sliced
- 1/2 cup sesame ginger salad dressing
- 6 cups baby kale salad blend (about 5 ounces)
- 3 clementines, peeled and segmented
- 1 cup fresh bean sprouts
- 2 cups shelled edamame (frozen) (almost 10 ounces), thawed

Directions:

1. Take a mixing bowl and mix all the ingredients in it.
2. Divide the salad mixture among six bowls.
3. Except for the salad dressing, top with the remaining ingredients.
4. Serve with a side of dressing.

Per serving: Calories: 317Kcal; Fat: 17 g; Carbs: 32 g; Protein: 13 g: Sodium: 355 mg

38. Cilantro Lime Shrimp

Preparation time: 30 minutes
Cooking time: 5-10 minutes
Servings: 4
Ingredients:

- 1/4 teaspoon ground cumin
- 1/4 teaspoon pepper
- 1/3 cup chopped fresh cilantro
- 1-1/2 teaspoons grated lime zest
- 1 pound uncooked shrimp (16-20 per pound), peeled and deveined
- Lime slices
- 1/3 cup lime juice
- 1 jalapeno pepper, seeded and minced
- 2 tablespoons olive oil
- 3 garlic cloves, minced
- 1/4 teaspoon salt

Directions:

1. Mix all ingredients except the lime slices with the shrimp. Allow 15 minutes for cooling.
2. Take 4 metal or soaked wooden skewers; thread shrimps and lime slices onto them.
3. Cover and grill until shrimp turn pink, about 2-4 minutes per side, over medium heat.

Per serving: Calories: 167 Kcal; Fat: 8 g; Carbs: 4 g; Protein: 19 g: Sodium: 284 mg

39. Sardines with Lemony Tomato Sauce

Preparation time: 25 minutes
Cooking time: 5-10 minutes
Servings: 4
Ingredients:

- 2 tablespoons olive oil, divided
- 4 Roma tomatoes, peeled and chopped, reserve the juice
- 1 small onion, sliced thinly
- Zest of 1 orange
- Sea salt and freshly ground pepper, to taste
- 1 pound (454 g) fresh sardines, rinsed, spine removed, butterflied
- ½ cup white wine
- 2 tablespoons whole-wheat breadcrumbs

Directions:

1. Preheat the oven to 425ºF (220ºC). Grease a baking dish with 1 tablespoon of olive oil.
2. Heat the remaining olive oil in a nonstick skillet over medium-low heat until simmering.
3. Add the tomatoes with juice, onion, orange zest, salt, and ground pepper to the skillet and simmer for 20 minutes or until it thickens.
4. Pour half of the mixture on the bottom of the baking dish, and then top with the butterflied sardines. Pour the remaining mixture and white wine over the sardines.
5. Spread the breadcrumbs on top, and then place the baking dish in the preheated oven. Bake for 20 minutes or until the fish is opaque.
6. Remove the baking sheet from the oven and serve the sardines warm.

Per serving: Calories: 370 Kcal; Fat: 15 g; Carbs: 39 g; Protein: 29 g; Sodium: 380 mg

40. Baby Potato and Olive Salad

Preparation time: 10 minutes
Cooking time: 20 minutes
Servings: 4
Ingredients:

- 2 tablespoons torn fresh mint
- 1 cup sliced celery (about 2 stalks)
- 2 tablespoons chopped fresh oregano
- 2 pounds (905 g) baby potatoes, cut into 1-inch cubes
- ¼ teaspoon kosher salt
- 3 tablespoons extra-virgin olive oil
- ½ cup sliced olives
- 1 tablespoon low-sodium olive brine

- 3 tablespoons lemon juice (fresh) (from about 1 medium lemon)

Directions:

1. Put the tomatoes in a saucepan, and then pour in enough water to submerge the tomatoes about 1 inch.

2. Bring them to a boil over high heat, and then reduce the heat to medium-low. Simmer for 14 minutes or until the potatoes are soft.

3. Meanwhile, combine the olive brine, lemon juice, salt, and olive oil in a small bow. Stir to mix well.

4. Transfer the cooked tomatoes in a colander, and then rinse with running cold water. Pat dry with paper towels.

5. Transfer the tomatoes in a large salad bowl, and then drizzle with olive brine mixture. Spread with remaining ingredients and toss to combine well.

6. Serve immediately.

Per serving: Calories: 322 Kcal; Fat: 3 g; Carbs: 70 g; Protein: 7 g: Sodium: 36 mg

Chapter 3: Sauces, Dips, and Dressings

41. Asparagus with Horseradish Dip

Preparation time: 15 minutes

Cooking time: 0 minutes

Servings: 16

Ingredients:

- 32 fresh asparagus spears (about 2 pounds), trimmed
- 1 cup reduced-fat mayonnaise
- 1/4 cup grated Parmesan cheese
- 1 tablespoon prepared horseradish
- 1/2 teaspoon Worcestershire sauce

Directions:

1. First, place the asparagus in a steamer basket in a big saucepan with 1 inch of water in it.
2. Bring it to a boil, and then reduce the flame to low and steam for 2-4 minutes, until crisp-tender.
3. Drain the asparagus and submerge in ice water as soon as possible. Afterwards, drain and dry.
4. Toss the remaining ingredients in a small mixing basin. Arrange asparagus on the sides.

Per serving: Calories: 63 Kcal; Fat: 5 g; Carbs: 3 g; Protein: 1 g: Sodium: 146 mg

42. Layered Hummus Dip

Preparation time: 15 minutes

Cooking time: 0 minutes

Servings: 12

Ingredients:

- 1 carton (10 ounces) hummus
- 1/4 cup finely chopped red onion
- 1/2 cup Greek olives, chopped
- 2 medium tomatoes, seeded and chopped
- 1 large English cucumber, chopped
- 1 cup crumbled feta cheese
- Baked pita chips

Directions:

1. In a shallow 10-inch round dish, spread the hummus out evenly.
2. Onion, olives, tomatoes, cucumber, and cheese are all layered on top of each other.
3. Chill until ready to serve. Pita chips should be served alongside.

Per serving: Calories: 88 Kcal; Fat: 5 g; Carbs: 6 g; Protein: 4 g: Sodium: 275 mg

43. Skinny Quinoa Veggie Dip

Preparation time: 20 minutes

Cooking time: 15 minutes

Servings: 15

Ingredients:

- ½ cup finely chopped zucchini
- ¾ teaspoon ground cumin
- ¼ teaspoon cayenne pepper
- ¾ cups water, divided
- Salt and pepper to taste
- 1/3 cup quinoa, rinsed
- 2 1/2 tablespoons lime juice, divided
- 1 medium ripe avocado, peeled and coarsely chopped
- 2 tablespoon plus 3/4 cup sour cream, divided
- 2 tbsp. minced fresh cilantro
- 1 1/2 plum tomatoes, chopped
- 3/4 teaspoons paprika
- 1/2 cup peeled, seeded and finely chopped cucumber
- 2 tbsp. finely chopped red onion
- 1 can (15 ounces) black beans, rinsed and drained
- Cucumber slices

Directions:

1. In a food processor, blend the beans, cumin, paprika, cayenne, and 1/3 cup water until smooth. Season to taste with salt and pepper.
2. In a small pot with the remaining 1-1/3 cup water, cook the quinoa according to instructions on packaging.
3. Sprinkle with 2 tablespoons of lime juice and fluff with fork. Remove from the equation.
4. Meanwhile, mash avocados with 2 tablespoons sour cream, cilantro, and the remaining lime juice in a mixing bowl.
5. Layer the bean mixture, avocado mixture, remaining sour cream, quinoa, tomatoes, diced cucumber, zucchini, and onion in a 2-1/2-quart dish.
6. Refrigerate or serve immediately with cucumber slices for dipping.

Per serving: Calories: 66 Kcal; Fat: 3 g; Carbs: 8 g; Protein: g: 2 Sodium: 54 mg

44. Dill Dip

Preparation time: 10 minutes

Cooking time: 0 minutes

Servings: 10

Ingredients:
- ½ cup low fat cottage cheese
- ½ tablespoon lemon juice
- 4 tbsp. skim milk (or less to reach desired consistency)
- ½ tsp. dash salt
- ½ tablespoon fresh dill, chopped
- ½ tablespoon onion, minced

Directions:
1. In a blender, combine cottage cheese, lemon juice, skim milk, and salt. Blend until creamy, adding more milk if necessary to achieve the desired consistency.
2. Add chopped fresh dill and minced onion to the mixture.
3. Chill and serve.

Per serving: Calories: 63 Kcal; Fat: 2.1 g; Carbs: 7 g; Protein: 1.8 g: Sodium: 49 mg

45. Low Sodium Spaghetti Sauce

Preparation time: 10 minutes

Cooking time: 0 minutes

Servings: ½ cup

Ingredients:
- 1/4 cup onions, chopped
- 15 oz. tomato sauce (no salt added) (canned)
- 8 tablespoon of no salt added tomato paste
- 1 1/2 tablespoon sugar
- 3 tsps. garlic, diced or minced
- 1 1/2 tsps. ground oregano
- 2 tbsps. leaves basil (dried)
- 1/8 tsp crushed red pepper flakes
- 1 1/2 cup of water

Directions:
1. Coat a non-stick pan using cooking spray. Set the heat to medium-low.
2. Add the onions and cook until they are transparent, and then add the tomato sauce and tomato paste, followed by the water.
3. Finally, stir in all the spices and cook for about30 minutes on low heat. Using the ground beef or not is up to you.

Per serving: Calories: 357 Kcal; Fat: 0 g; Carbs: 8 g; Protein: 1 g: Sodium: 26 mg

46. Avocado Dip

Preparation time: 10 minutes

Cooking time: 0 minutes

Servings: 8

Ingredients:
- 4 teaspoons chopped onion
- 1/4 teaspoon hot sauce
- 2 ripe avocados, peeled, pitted and mashed (about 1/2 cup)
- 1 cup fat-free sour cream

Directions:

1. Mix the sour cream, onion, spicy sauce, and avocado together in a small bowl.
2. To ensure that the components are evenly distributed, combine them in a mixing bowl.
3. Serve with sliced vegetables or tortilla chips cooked in the oven.

Per serving: Calories: Kcal; 85 Fat: 5 g; Carbs: 8 g; Protein: 2 g: Sodium: 57 mg

47. Avocado Salsa

Preparation time: 10 minutes

Cooking time: 0 minutes

Servings: 20

Ingredients:

- 5 Roma tomatoes, chopped
- 3 avocados, cubed
- 1/2 chopped red onion
- 2 tablespoons chopped cilantro
- 2 cloves garlic, minced
- 1/2 lime, juiced
- 1/4 teaspoon salt
- Ground black pepper, to taste

Directions:

1. Toss the tomatoes, avocados, red onion, cilantro, and garlic in a medium mixing basin.
2. Add lime juice to the mixture and season with salt and pepper. Lime juice should be added now. Serve after a thorough mixing.

Per serving: Calories: 41 Kcal; Fat: 0 g; Carbs: 3 g; Protein: 1 g: Sodium: 62 mg

48. Cilantro Lime Dressing

Preparation time: 10 minutes

Cooking time: 0 minutes

Servings:

Ingredients:

- 1/4 cup olive oil
- 2 cups 1 percent cottage cheese

- 1 clove garlic
- 2 whole limes, juiced
- 1/2 teaspoon salt
- 1/2 cup cilantro, roughly chopped
- 1/2 teaspoon sugar
- 1/4 teaspoon ground black pepper

Directions:

1. All of the ingredients should be combined in a food processor or blender. Blend until the mixture is smooth.
2. Serve and enjoy.

Per serving: Calories: 54 Kcal; Fat: 4 g; Carbs: 2 g; Protein: 4 g: Sodium: 190 mg

49. House Ranch Dressing

Preparation time: 10 minutes

Cooking time: 0 minutes

Servings: 20

Ingredients:

- 2 cups plain fat-free Greek yogurt
- 1/2 cup low-fat mayonnaise
- 2 tablespoons lemon juice
- 1 tablespoon dried dill weed
- 1/2 tablespoon onion powder
- 1/2 tablespoon garlic powder
- 1/2 teaspoon kosher salt
- 1/4 teaspoon black pepper

Directions:

1. All ingredients should be combined in a food processor and processed until uniformly distributed.
2. Stop the food processor if necessary to scrape the sides.
3. Serve right away or you can keep in refrigerator for up to 2 weeks in a plastic container.

Per serving: Calories: 30 Kcal; Fat: 1 g; Carbs: 2 g; Protein: 2 g: Sodium: 110 mg

50. Italian Salad Dressing

Preparation time: 10 minutes

Cooking time: 0 minutes

Servings: 3

Ingredients:

- 3 tablespoons olive oil
- 2 tablespoons red wine vinegar
- 1 tablespoon lemon juice
- 2 teaspoons Dijon mustard
- 1 clove garlic, minced
- 1 teaspoon dried parsley
- 1 teaspoon dried basil, crumbled
- 1/8 teaspoon dried oregano
- 1/8 teaspoon crushed red pepper flakes

Directions:

1. Take a screw-top jar and combine all ingredients.
2. Shake the jar to combine.
3. Cover and store in the refrigerator.

Per serving: Calories: 50 Kcal; Fat: 5 g; Carbs: 2 g; Protein: 1 g: Sodium: 30 mg

51. Mango Salsa

Preparation time: 10 minutes

Cooking time: 0 minutes

Servings: 2

Ingredients:

- 1 mango, diced (about 1 cup)
- 1/4 small red onion, minced (
- 1 ½ red Fresno peppers, minced
- 1 tablespoon minced cilantro
- Zest and juice of ½ lime
- ½ tablespoon olive oil

Directions:

1. Add all the ingredients in a mixing bowl. Give it a good mix and it is ready to be served.

Per serving: Calories: 101 Kcal; Fat: 0.5 g; Carbs: 15 g; Protein: 1 g: Sodium: 3 mg

52. Peach Honey Spread

Preparation time: 10 minutes

Cooking time: 0 minutes

Servings: 4

Ingredients:

- 1 can (15 ounces) unsweetened peach, halved, drained
- 2 tablespoons honey
- 1/2 teaspoon cinnamon

Directions:

1. Combine the honey, cinnamon, and peaches in a large mixing bowl. Mash the ingredients with a fork until it resembles chunky apple sauce.
2. Serve right away, or cover and chill until ready to serve.

Per serving: Calories: 60 Kcal; Fat: 0 g; Carbs: 14 g; Protein: 0.5 g: Sodium: 3 mg

53. Peanut Butter Hummus

Preparation time: 10 minutes

Cooking time: minutes

Servings: 16

Ingredients:

- 2 cups garbanzo beans
- 1 cup water
- 1/2 cup powdered peanut butter
- 1/4 cup natural peanut butter
- 2 tablespoons brown sugar
- 1 teaspoon vanilla extract

Directions:

1. For making peanut butter hummus, combine all the ingredients in a food processor. Blend until the mixture is completely smooth. Refrigerate for up to a week in the refrigerator.

Per serving: Calories: 135 Kcal; Fat: 4 g; Carbs: 20g; Protein: 7 g: Sodium: 47 mg

54. Pepper Sauce

Preparation time: 10 minutes

Cooking time: 30 minutes

Servings: 10

Ingredients:

- 1 dried ancho chili pepper
- 1 dried chipotle chili pepper
- 1 dried New Mexico chili pepper
- 1/2 cup water

- 1 cup white wine vinegar
- 1 fresh red Fresno or jalapeno chili pepper
- 1/4 cup olive oil

Directions:

1. Remove the stems and seeds from dried and fresh chilies with gloves. For one hour, soak dried pepper in vinegar and water.
2. In a sauce pan, combine the peppers and liquid. Simmer for 30 minutes over low heat with fresh Fresno chile (or jalapeno).
3. Now remove the pan from the heat and set aside to cool.
4. Puree in a blender until completely smooth. Slowly sprinkle in the oil while the mixer is running. Refrigerate any leftovers.

Per serving: Calories: 65 Kcal; Fat: 6 g; Carbs: 2 g; Protein: 0.5 g: Sodium: 3 mg

55. Savory Vegetable Dip

Preparation time: 10 minutes

Cooking time: 0 minutes

Servings: 10

Ingredients:

- 2/3 cup plain fat-free yogurt
- 1 1/2 cups chopped sun-dried tomatoes, dried and drained
- 2 cups fat-free cottage cheese
- 2/3 cup fat-free mayonnaise
- 6 cloves garlic, peeled and cut in half

Directions:

1. Blend the ingredients in a food processor until smooth.
2. Serve with your favorite vegetables after chilling for 3 hours or overnight.

Per serving: Calories: 57 Kcal; Fat: 1.5 g; Carbs: 7 g; Protein: 4 g: Sodium: 223 mg

56. Vegetable salsa

Preparation time: 10 minutes

Cooking time: 5 minutes

Servings: 8

Ingredients:

- 1 red bell pepper, seeded and diced (about 2 cups)
- 1 teaspoon sugar
- 1/8 cup lime juice
- 1 green bell pepper, seeded and diced (about 2 cups)
- 2 tomatoes, diced (about 2 cups)
- 1 garlic cloves, minced
- 1/2 cup diced zucchini
- 1/2 cup chopped red onion
- 1/4 cup chopped fresh cilantro
- 1/2 teaspoon ground black pepper
- 1/4 teaspoon salt

Directions:

1. Prepare the vegetables by washing them according to the package directions.
2. Combine all of the ingredients in a large mixing basin.
3. To combine the ingredients, gently toss them together. To enable the flavors to mix, cover and chill for at least 30 minutes.

Per serving: Calories: 24 Kcal; Fat: 0 g; Carbs: 5 g; Protein: 1 g: Sodium: 80 mg

57. Mushroom Sauce

Preparation time: 10 minutes

Cooking time: 10 minutes

Servings: 12

Ingredients:

- 2 cups fat-free milk
- 2 teaspoons canola oil
- 1 small onion, diced
- 1 1/2 cups sliced fresh mushrooms
- 2 tablespoons all-purpose flour
- 1 tablespoon chopped chives
- Ground black pepper, to taste
- 1 teaspoon sherry (optional)

Directions:

1. To warm the milk, add it to a small saucepan over low heat.
2. Heat the canola oil in a nonstick skillet over medium heat.
3. Sauté for 3 minutes after adding the onions. Sauté for another 3 minutes with the sliced mushrooms.
4. Cook for another 2 to 3 minutes after adding the flour.
5. Add the warmed milk and whisk to combine. Cooking should be for 3 minutes, stirring often until the sauce has thickened. If desired, garnish with chives, pepper, and sherry. Warm the mushroom sauce over low heat until ready to serve.

Per serving: Calories: 35 Kcal; Fat: 1 g; Carbs: 4 g; Protein: 2 g: Sodium: 19 mg

58. Spinach Dip with Mushrooms

Preparation time: 10 minutes

Cooking time: 0 minutes

Servings: 10

Ingredients:

- 1 package of chopped spinach (frozen) (10 ounces), thawed and squeezed dry
- 1 1/2 cups fat-free sour cream
- 1 cup fat-free mayonnaise
- 1 cup chopped fresh mushrooms
- 3 green onions, chopped

Directions:

1. Combine all ingredients in a medium-sized mixing bowl.
2. Mix the ingredients, cover, and chill. Serve with a variety of raw veggies, chilled.

Per serving: Calories: 55 Kcal; Fat: 0 g; Carbs: 11 g; Protein: 3 g: Sodium: 270 mg

59. Blue Cheese Dressing

Preparation time: 10 minutes

Cooking time: 0 minutes

Servings: 16

Ingredients:

- 1/2 cup blue cheese crumbles
- 1 tablespoon minced garlic
- 1 cup fat-free mayonnaise
- 1 tablespoon horseradish
- 1 teaspoon Worcestershire sauce
- 1/2 cup low-fat buttermilk
- 1/2 teaspoon cayenne pepper

Directions:

1. In a blender or food processor, combine all of the ingredients. Chill before serving.

Per serving: Calories: 32 Kcal; Fat: 2 g; Carbs: 2.5 g; Protein: 1 g: Sodium: 173 mg

60. Cilantro Lime Dressing

Preparation time: 10 minutes

Cooking time: 0 minutes

Servings: 16

Ingredients:

- 1/4 cup olive oil
- 2 cups 1 percent cottage cheese
- 1 clove garlic
- 2 whole limes, juiced
- 1/2 teaspoon salt
- 1/2 cup cilantro, roughly chopped
- 1/2 teaspoon sugar
- 1/4 teaspoon ground black pepper

Directions:

1. Combine all the ingredients in a food processor. Blend until completely smooth.

Per serving: Calories: 55 Kcal; Fat: g; 4 Carbs: 2 g; Protein: 4 g: Sodium: 190 mg

Chapter 4: Beans and Grains

61. Mexican Bake

Preparation time: 15 minutes

Cooking time: 45 minutes

Servings: 6

Ingredients:

- 1 cup frozen yellow corn kernels
- 1 cup shredded reduced-fat cheese
- 2 (14.5 ounce) cans no-salt-added tomatoes, diced or crushed
- ¼ cup jalapeno pepper slices (Optional)
- 1 cup chopped red bell pepper
- 1 cup chopped poblano pepper
- 1 ½ cups cooked rice, preferably brown
- 1 (15 ounce) can no-salt-added black beans, drained and rinsed
- 1 tablespoon chili powder
- 1 tablespoon cumin
- 4 garlic cloves, crushed
- 1 pound boneless chicken breast, skinless cut in bite-sized pieces

Directions:

1. First, preheat the oven to 400 degrees F.
2. In a 3-quart shallow casserole, spread the rice out evenly and chicken on top.
3. Combine the tomatoes, beans, corn, peppers, spices, and garlic in a mixing bowl and pour over the chicken. You can add Cheese and jalapeno, to go on top if desired.
4. Bake for 45 minutes and serve.

Per serving: Calories: 325 Kcal; Fat: 7 g; Carbs 37: g; Protein: 28 g: Sodium: 355 mg

62. Cannellini Bean Hummus

Preparation time: 5 minutes

Cooking time: 0 minutes

Servings: 10

Ingredients:

- Pita breads, cut into wedges
- Assorted fresh vegetables
- 2 garlic cloves, peeled
- 1 can (15 ounces) cannellini beans, rinsed and drained
- 1/4 cup tahini
- 1/4 teaspoon salt
- 1/4 teaspoon crushed red pepper flakes
- 2 tablespoons minced fresh parsley
- 3 tablespoons lemon juice
- 1-1/2 teaspoons ground cumin

Directions:

1. Place the garlic in a food processor and pulse until it is minced. Cover and pulse until smooth, then add the beans, tahini, lemon juice, cumin, salt, and pepper flakes.
2. Stir in the parsley in a small bowl. Chill until ready to serve. Assorted fresh vegetables and pita wedges

Per serving: Calories: 78 Kcal; Fat: 4 g; Carbs: 8 g; Protein: 3 g: Sodium: 114 mg

63. Black Bean & White Cheddar Frittata

Preparation time: 20 minutes

Cooking time: 15 minutes

Servings: 6

Ingredients:

- 1/3 cup finely chopped sweet red pepper
- 3 green onions, finely chopped
- 1 cup canned black beans, rinsed and drained
- 1/2 cup shredded white cheddar cheese
- 6 large eggs
- 3 large egg whites
- 1/4 cup salsa
- 1 tablespoon olive oil
- 2 garlic cloves, minced

- 1 tablespoon minced fresh parsley
- 1/4 teaspoon salt
- 1/4 teaspoon pepper
- 1/3 cup finely chopped green pepper
- Options for toppings: Minced fresh cilantro, sliced ripe olives and additional salsa

Directions:

1. Preheat the oven to broil. In a large bowl, mix the first 6 ingredients until combined.
2. Heat oil in a 10-inch ovenproof skillet over medium-high heat.
3. Add the peppers and green onions and simmer, stirring occasionally, for 3-4 minutes, or until the peppers are soft.
4. Cook for a further minute after adding the garlic. Add the beans and mix well. Reduce the heat to medium-low and whisk in the egg mixture.
5. Cook for 4-6 minutes, uncovered, or until nearly set. Spread the cheese on top.
6. After 3-4 minutes, or when light golden brown and eggs are totally set, broil 3-4 inches from flame. Allow for a 5-minute rest period. Cut the wedges in half. Garnish with toppings as desired.

Per serving: Calories: 180 Kcal; Fat: 10 g; Carbs: 9 g; Protein: 13 g: Sodium: 380 mg

64. Black Bean & Sweet Potato Rice Bowls

Preparation time: 10 minutes

Cooking time: 30 minutes

Servings: 8

Ingredients:

- 1 ½ cups uncooked long grain rice
- 1/2 teaspoon garlic salt
- 2 medium red onions, finely chopped
- 8 cups chopped fresh kale (tough stems removed)
- 2 cans black beans, rinsed and drained
- 3 cups water
- 6 tablespoons olive oil, divided

- 4 tablespoons sweet chili sauce
- 2 large sweet potatoes, peeled and diced
- Lime wedges and additional sweet chili sauce (optional)

Directions:

1. In a large saucepan, combine the rice, garlic salt, and water; bring to a boil. Reduce heat to low; cover and cook for 15-20 minutes, or until water is absorbed and rice is soft. Remove from the heat and let aside for 5 minutes.
2. Meanwhile, heat 2 tablespoons oil in a large skillet over medium-high heat and sauté sweet potato for 8 minutes.
3. Cook and stir until the potato is tender, about 4-6 minutes. Cook, stirring frequently, until the kale is soft, about 3-5 minutes. Add the beans and heat thoroughly.
4. Add 2 tablespoons chili sauce and remaining oil, gently stirred into rice; add to potato mixture. Serve with lime wedges and more chili sauce, if preferred.

Per serving: Calories: 435 Kcal; Fat: 11 g; Carbs: 75 g; Protein: 10 g: Sodium: 402mg

65. White Beans & Bow Ties

Preparation time: 15 minutes

Cooking time: 10 minutes

Servings: 4

Ingredients:

- 1 1/2 teaspoon freshly ground pepper
- 1 cup crumbled feta cheese
- 2 tablespoons olive oil
- 4 large tomatoes, chopped (about 2-1/2 cups)
- 2 cans (15 ounces) cannellini beans, rinsed and drained
- 2 cans (2-1/4 ounces) sliced ripe olives, drained
- 2 medium zucchinis, sliced
- 4 garlic cloves, minced

- 5 cups uncooked whole wheat bow tie pasta (about 6 ounces)

Directions:

1. Cook the pasta as directed on the packet. Drain the pasta, reserving 1/2 cup of the water.
2. Meanwhile, heat the oil in a large skillet over medium-high heat and cook the zucchini until crisp-tender, about 2-4 minutes.
3. Cook and stir for 30 seconds after adding the garlic. Bring to a boil with the tomatoes, beans, olives, and pepper.
4. Reduce heat to low and cook, uncovered, for 3-5 minutes, or until tomatoes are softened, stirring periodically.
5. Take a large sized mixing bowl; combine the pasta and enough pasta water to moisten as needed. Add the cheese and mix well.

Per serving: Calories: 350 Kcal; Fat: 9 g; Carbs: 395 g; Protein: 15 g: Sodium: 395 mg

66. Black Bean and Corn Relish

Preparation time: 10 minutes
Cooking time: 0 minutes
Servings: 8
Ingredients:

- 1/2 medium red onion, diced (about 1/2 cup)
- 1/2 cup of chopped parsley
- 2 teaspoons sugar
- 2 garlic cloves, chopped
- Juice from 1 lemon
- 1 can black beans, rinsed and drained (almost 2 cups)
- 1 green/yellow/red bell pepper, seeded and diced (almost 1 cup)
- 1 cup frozen corn kernels, thawed to room temperature
- 4 tomatoes, seeded and diced (almost 3 cups)

Directions:

1. Combine the ingredients in a large mixing bowl.
2. Toss gently to combine the ingredients. To mix the flavors, cover and chill for at least 30 minutes.

Per serving: Calories: 112 Kcal; Fat: 0.5 g; Carbs: 22 g; Protein: 5 g: Sodium: 94mg

67. Gluten-Free Hummus

Preparation time: 25 minutes
Cooking time: 50-60 minutes
Servings: 6
Ingredients:

- 3 tablespoons chopped fresh cilantro (fresh coriander)
- 1 teaspoon ground cumin
- 2 tablespoons sherry vinegar
- 2/3 cup dried chickpeas, picked over and rinsed, soaked overnight, and drained
- 3 cups water
- 1/2 teaspoon salt
- 1 tablespoon olive oil
- 2 cloves garlic
- 1 bay leaf
- 3/4 cup & 2 tablespoons sliced green onion

Directions:

1. First, combine the chickpeas, water, garlic cloves, bay leaf, and 1/4 teaspoon salt in a large pot over high heat.
2. Raise the temperature to high and bring the mixture to a boil. Reduce to a low heat, partially cover, and cook for 50 to 60 minutes, or until the beans are very soft. The bay leaf should be discarded, but the garlic and 1/2 cup of the cooking liquid should be saved.
3. Then combine chickpeas, vinegar, olive oil, 3/4 cup green onion, cooked garlic, cilantro, cumin, and the remaining 1/4 teaspoon salt in a blender or food

processor and blend or process until smooth.

4. Blend until smooth. 1 tablespoon at a time, add the remaining cooking liquid until the mixture reaches a thick spreadable consistency.

5. Combine the chickpea mixture with the remaining 2 tablespoons green onion in a small serving bowl and toss to combine. Serve right away, chill it covered until ready to use.

Per serving: Calories: Kcal; Fat: g; Carbs: g; Protein: g: Sodium: mg

68. Hummus

Preparation time: 10 minutes

Cooking time: 0 minutes

Servings: 14

Ingredients:

- 3 tablespoons tahini (sesame paste)
- 2 tablespoons chopped Italian flat-leaf parsley
- 2 cans reduced-sodium chickpeas, rinsed and drained (almost 16 ounces each)
- 1 tablespoon extra-virgin olive oil
- 1/4 teaspoon cracked black pepper
- 1/4 teaspoon paprika
- 1/4 cup lemon juice
- 2 garlic cloves, minced

Directions:

1. To purée the chickpeas, use a blender or food processor. Combine the olive oil, lemon juice, garlic, pepper, paprika, tahini, and parsley in a large mixing bowl. Make a thorough mixture.

2. 1 tablespoon at a time, add the reserved liquid until the mixture reaches a thick spreadable consistency.

3. Serve right away, or cover and chill until ready to use.

Per serving: Calories: 89 Kcal; Fat: 4 g; Carbs: 9 g; Protein: 4 g: Sodium: 80 mg

69. Peanut Butter Hummus

Preparation time: 15 minutes

Cooking time: 0 minutes

Servings: 16

Ingredients:

- 1/2 cup powdered peanut butter
- 1/4 cup natural peanut butter
- 2 cups garbanzo beans
- 1 cup water
- 2 tablespoons brown sugar
- 1 teaspoon vanilla extract

Directions:

1. In a food processor, combine all of the ingredients.

2. Blend until completely smooth. Refrigerate for up to a week before serving.

Per serving: Calories: 135 Kcal; Fat: 4 g; Carbs: 20 g; Protein: 7 g: Sodium: 48 mg

70. White Bean Dip

Preparation time: 10 minutes

Cooking time: 0 minutes

Servings: 8

Ingredients:

- 2 tablespoons olive oil
- 2 tablespoons lemon juice
- 1 can (15 ounces) white (cannellini) beans, rinsed and drained
- 8 garlic cloves, roasted

Directions:

1. Mix the beans, roasted garlic, olive oil, and lemon juice together in a blender or food processor. Blend until smooth.

2. Serve with pita triangles or thinly sliced toasted French bread. This works well on top of cut-up red (sweet) bell peppers.

Per serving: Calories: 84 Kcal; Fat: 4 g; Carbs: 9 g; Protein: 3 g: Sodium: 125 mg

71. Bean Salad with Balsamic Vinaigrette

Preparation time: 20 minutes
Cooking time: 0 minutes
Servings: 6
Ingredients:

For the vinaigrette:

- Ground black pepper, to taste
- 1/4 cup extra-virgin olive oil
- 2 tablespoons balsamic vinegar
- 1/3 cup fresh parsley, chopped
- 4 garlic cloves, finely chopped

For the salad:

- 1 medium sized red onion, diced
- 6 lettuce leaves
- 1 can low-sodium garbanzo beans, rinsed and drained (15 ounces almost)
- 1/2 cup celery, finely chopped
- 1 can low-sodium black beans, rinsed and drained

Directions:

1. First, whisk together the vinegar, parsley, garlic, and pepper in a small bowl to make the vinaigrette. Slowly drizzle in the olive oil as you stir. Remove the item from circulation.
2. Toss the beans and onion in a large mixing dish. Pour the vinaigrette over the salad and gently toss to coat everything evenly. Refrigerate until ready to serve, covered.
3. Place one lettuce leaf each plate to serve.
4. Serve the salad on individual plates with sliced celery on top.

Per serving: Calories: 205 Kcal; Fat: 1 g; Carbs: 22 g; Protein: 7 g: Sodium: 175 mg

72. Whole-Grain Pancakes

Preparation time: 15 minutes
Cooking time: 15 minutes
Servings: 9

Ingredients:

- 2 1/4 cups soy milk
- 3 large egg whites, beaten
- 1 cup whole-wheat flour
- 1/4 cup millet flour
- 1/2 cup barley flour
- 2 tablespoons flaxseed flour
- 3 tablespoons honey
- 1 tablespoon oil
- 1/4 cup rolled oats
- 1 1/2 tablespoons baking powder

Directions:

1. In a large dish, combine dry ingredients together.
2. Combine the wet ingredients — honey, oil, soy milk, and beaten egg whites — in a separate bowl. Add egg mixture to dry ingredients. Stir until everything is well blended. Allow 30 minutes for the batter to rest in the refrigerator.
3. Preheat the oven to 225 degrees Fahrenheit and place a baking sheet inside. Preheat a frying pan over medium-high heat.
4. To prepare one pancake, spoon or ladle roughly 1/4 cup of batter into the pan. Cook until little bubbles appear and the edges appear dry.
5. Cook until the second side is golden brown. To keep the pancake warm, place it on a baking sheet.
6. Continue with the remaining batter.
7. Serve with fresh fruit or a small sprinkling of powdered sugar on top.

Per serving: Calories: 180 Kcal; Fat: 1 g; Carbs: 30 g; Protein: 6 g: Sodium: 170 mg

73. Quick Bean and Tuna Salad

Preparation time: 20 minutes
Cooking time: 5 minutes
Servings: 4
Ingredients:

- 1/4 teaspoon pepper
- 1 can (7 ounces) water-packed tuna, no salt added, drained and rinsed
- 2 tablespoons finely chopped fresh parsley
- 1/2 whole-grain baguette, torn into 2-inch pieces (about 1 cup)
- 2 tablespoons olive oil
- 1 can (16 ounces) cannellini beans, no salt added, drained and rinsed
- 1 small red onion, thinly sliced (about 1/2 cup)
- 2 tablespoons red wine vinegar
- 2 small dill pickles, cut into bite-size pieces (about 2 tablespoons)

Directions:

1. Preheat the broiler. Brush 1 tablespoon of the oil over the baguette slices on a sturdy cookie sheet.
2. Place under the broiler for 1–2 minutes, or until golden brown.
3. Broil for a further 1 or 2 minutes after turning the bread pieces.
4. In a large bowl, add the remaining oil, beans, pickles, onion, vinegar, and pepper. Fold in the pieces of broiled baguette.
5. Top with tuna and parsley and divide the mixture among four bowls.

Per serving: Calories: 31 Kcal; Fat: 10 g; Carbs: 23 g; Protein: 19 g: Sodium: 171 mg

74. Rice and Beans Salad

Preparation time: 15 minutes

Cooking time: 50 minutes

Servings: 10

Ingredients:

- 1/4 cup olive oil
- 1 1/2 cups uncooked brown rice
- 1/2 cup shallots or spring onions, chopped
- 15-ounce can unsalted garbanzo beans
- 3 cups water
- 1/2 cup chopped fresh parsley

- 1/3 cup rice vinegar, to your taste
- 15-ounce can unsalted dark kidney beans

Directions:

1. In a stockpot, combine rice and water. Cover and cook over medium heat for 45 to 50 minutes, or until rice is soft.
2. Bring to room temperature before serving.
3. Combine the remaining ingredients in a mixing bowl. Chill for at least 2 hours.

Per serving: Calories: 227 Kcal; Fat: 7 g; Carbs: 34 g; Protein: 7 g: Sodium: 110mg

75. Black Bean Wrap

Preparation time: 15 minutes

Cooking time: 5 minutes

Servings: 6

Ingredients:

- 3/4 cup shredded cheddar cheese
- 3/4 cup salsa
- 1 1/2 cups low-sodium black beans, rinsed, canned and drained
- 4 green onions, diced (including green stems)
- 1 tomato, diced
- 1 tablespoon chopped garlic
- 3 tablespoons chopped fresh cilantro
- 2 tablespoons green chili peppers, chopped and seeds removed
- 6 fat-free whole-grain tortilla wraps, 10 inches in diameter
- 1 1/2 cups frozen corn kernels, thawed to room temperature

Directions:

1. First, add the chili peppers, corn, cilantro, black beans, onions, tomato, and garlic to a microwave-safe bowl and mix well.
2. To ensure a uniform distribution of ingredients, stir them together. 30 seconds to 1 minute in a high-powered microwave.

3. Heat for 30 seconds to 1 minute after stirring. Continue until the mixture reaches a boiling point.
4. Warm 2 tortillas in the microwave for 20 seconds on high, sandwiched between paper napkins or paper towels. Using the remaining tortillas, repeat the process.
5. Place roughly 1/2 cup bean mixture on each tortilla to serve. 2 tbsp. cheese, 2 tbsp. salsa Fold in the edges and fold the bottom of the tortilla up over the filling before rolling it up to close.
6. Continue with the remaining tortillas and serve right away.

Per serving: Calories: 340 Kcal; Fat: 9 g; Carbs: 50 g; Protein: 15 g: Sodium: 630 mg

76. Hot 6-Grain Cereal

Preparation time: 10 minutes
Cooking time: 45 minutes
Servings: 7
Ingredients:
- 2 tablespoons of flaxseed
- 1/2 teaspoon kosher salt
- 1 1/2 quarts water
- 1/2 cup uncooked pearl barley
- 1/2 cup uncooked red wheat berries
- 3 tablespoons uncooked quinoa
- 1/2 cup uncooked brown rice
- 1/4 cup uncooked steel cut oats

Directions:
1. Toss the barley, wheat berries, rice, oats, quinoa, flaxseed, and salt together in a large pot.
2. Pour water over ingredients, stir, and bring to a boil over medium heat.
3. Reduce to a low heat and cook, stirring periodically, for 45 minutes.

Per serving: Calories: 115 Kcal; Fat: 1 g; Carbs: 21 g; Protein: 4 g: Sodium: 75 mg

77. Turkish Canned Pinto Bean Salad

Preparation time: 10 minutes
Cooking time: 25 minutes
Servings: 6
Ingredients:
- 2 Large hard-cooked eggs quartered
- 1 Tablespoon toasted sesame seeds
- 1/4 Cup extra virgin-olive oil.
- 3 Garlic cloves lightly crushed and peeled.
- 1 Cup (6 Ounces) orchard choice
- 1/2 Red onion thinly sliced
- 1/2 Cup fresh parsley leaves
- 2 (15 Ounce) cans pinto beans rinsed.
- Salt and pepper
- 1/4 Cup tahini
- 3 Tablespoons Lemon Juice
- 1 Tablespoon ground dried aleppo pepper
- 8 Ounces cherry tomatoes halved

Directions:
1. In a medium saucepan over medium heat, cook 1 tablespoon oil, and garlic, stirring frequently, for 3 minutes, or until garlic turns golden but not brown.
2. Bring to a low simmer with the beans, 2 cups water, and 1 teaspoon salt. Remove from the heat and let aside for 20 minutes, covered.
3. Remove the garlic cloves and drain the beans.
4. In a large mixing bowl, combine the remaining 3 tablespoons oil, the tahini, the lemon juice, the Aleppo pepper, 1 tablespoon water, and 1/4 teaspoon salt.
5. Gently stir together the beans, tomatoes, figs, onion, and parsley.
6. Season to taste with salt and pepper. Place the eggs on top of the potatoes on a serving plate. Serve with additional Aleppo pepper and sesame seeds on top.

Per serving: Calories: 331 Kcal; Fat: 12 g; Carbs: 46 g; Protein: 12 g: Sodium: 245 mg

78. Shrimp with Black Bean Pasta

Preparation time: 10 minutes

Cooking time: 15 minutes

Servings: 4

Ingredients:

- Salt and pepper, to taste.
- ¾ Cup low-sodium chicken broth.
- ¼ Cup basil, cut into strips.
- 1 Package black bean pasta.
- 1 Onion, finely chopped.
- 1 Pound (454 G) fresh shrimp peeled and deveined.
- 4 Tablespoons olive oil.
- 3 Garlic cloves, minced.

Directions:

1. In a large saucepan of boiling water, cook the black bean pasta for 6 minutes.
2. Turn off the heat and take the pasta off the stove. Drain the pasta and rinse it in cool water before placing it on a serving plate.
3. In a large skillet over medium heat, heat the olive oil. Cook for 3 minutes, until the onion is transparent, before adding the garlic and onion.
4. Season with salt and pepper before adding the shrimp. Cook for 3 minutes, or until the shrimp are opaque, stirring periodically. Pour in the chicken broth and cook for 2 to 3 minutes, or until well heated.
5. Transfer the shrimp to a dish of spaghetti and remove from the heat. Finish by pouring the liquid over the pasta and garnishing with parsley.

Per serving: Calories: 670 Kcal; Fat: 19 g; Carbs: 73 g; Protein: 55 g: Sodium: 612 mg

79. Rustic Lentil and Basmati Rice Pilaf

Preparation time: 5 minutes

Cooking time: 50 minutes

Servings: 6

Ingredients:

- 6 Cups of water.
- 2 Cups brown lentils, picked over, and rinsed.
- 1 cup basmati rice.
- ¼ Cup olive oil.
- 1 Large onion, chopped.
- 1 Teaspoon salt.
- 1 Teaspoon ground cumin.

Directions:

1. First, heat the olive oil in a saucepan over medium heat. Then, cook for about 4 minutes, or until the onions have turned a medium golden color.
2. Add the cumin, salt, and water to a high-heat pan. Allow the mixture to boil for 3 minutes, or until it is well heated.
3. Lower the heat to low and stir in the brown lentils. Allow to simmer, covered, for about 20 minutes, or until vegetables are soft.
4. Stir in the basmati rice thoroughly. Cook for 20 minutes, or until the rice has completely absorbed the liquid.
5. Fluff the rice with a fork, cover, and set aside for 5 minutes.
6. Arrange on plates and serve immediately.

Per serving: Calories: 400 Kcal; Fat: 11 g; Carbs: 59 g; Protein: 18 g: Sodium: 399 mg

80. Quick Spanish Rice

Preparation time: 10 minutes

Cooking time: 15 minutes

Servings: 4

Ingredients:

- 1½ Cups basmati rice
- 1 Teaspoon salt

- 3 Cups water
- 2 Tablespoons olive oil
- 1 Medium onion, finely chopped
- 1 Large tomato, finely diced
- 2 Tablespoons tomato paste
- 1 Teaspoon smoked paprika

Directions:

1. In a saucepan over medium heat, heat the olive oil. Add the onions and tomato and Sauté for about 3 minutes, or until they are softened.

2. Combine the paprika, tomato paste, basmati rice, and salt in a medium mixing bowl. Stir for 1 minute before adding the water slowly.

3. Reduce the heat to low and cook for 12 minutes, covered, stirring regularly.

4. Take it off the heat and set it aside for 3 minutes in the pot.

5. Serve the rice in four bowls, evenly divided.

Per serving: Calories: 331 Kcal; Fat: 7 g; Carbs: 59 g; Protein: 6 g: Sodium: 650 mg

Chapter 5: Vegetarian Recipes

81. Minestrone Soup

Preparation time: 15 minutes

Cooking time: 30 minutes

Servings: 3

Ingredients:

- 1/2 cup Pasta, macaroni, elbow, whole wheat, dry (choice of whole wheat pasta)
- 2 tbsp Basil, fresh (chopped)
- 1 small Zucchini (diced)
- 1 tbsp. Extra virgin olive oil
- 1/2 cup Yellow onion (chopped)
- 1 clove(s) Garlic (minced)
- 4 cup Chicken broth (stock), low sodium
- 2 large Tomato (seeded, chopped)
- 1/2 cup Spinach (chopped)
- 1/3 cup diced Celery
- 1 medium Carrots (diced)
- 1 can (15oz) Chickpeas, canned, low sodium (drained, rinsed)

Directions:

1. Heat the olive oil in a large saucepan over medium heat.
2. Add the onion, celery, and carrots and cook for 5 minutes, or until softened.
3. Stir in the garlic and simmer for another minute.
4. Combine the broth, tomatoes, spinach, beans, and pasta in a large mixing bowl.
5. Over high heat, bring to a boil. Reduce heat to low and cook for 10 minutes.
6. Toss in the zucchini. Cook for another 5 minutes, covered.

Per serving: Calories: 287 Kcal; Fat: 8.2 g; Carbs: 3 g; Protein: 18 g: Sodium: 839 mg

82. Swiss Chard Egg Drop Soup

Preparation time: 20 minutes

Cooking time: 10 minutes

Servings: 4

Ingredients:

- 2 tablespoons coconut aminos
- 1 teaspoon ginger, grated
- 3 cups bone broth
- 2 cups Swiss chard, chopped
- Salt and black pepper, to taste
- 2 eggs, whisked
- 1 teaspoon ground oregano
- 3 tablespoons butter

Directions:

1. In a saucepan, warm the bone broth and slowly whisk in the whisked eggs.
2. Combine the swiss chard, butter, coconut aminos, ginger, oregano, and salt and pepper in a large mixing bowl.
3. Cook for 10 minutes, and then serve immediately.

Per serving: Calories: 185 Kcal; Fat: 11 g; Carbs: g; 3 Protein: 18 g: Sodium: 250 mg

83. Roasted Veggies and Brown Rice Bowl

Preparation time: 15 minutes

Cooking time: 30 minutes

Servings: 4

Ingredients:

Veggies and Grains:

- 2 Cups cooked chickpeas or 1 can, rinsed and drained
- 2 Tbsp sesame seeds
- 1 Head cauliflower, cut into bite-size pieces
- 1 Cup brown rice
- 2 Tsp extra virgin olive oil
- Salt/Pepper

- 1 Head broccoli, cut into bite-size pieces
- 3 Medium carrots, cut into coins

Creamy Sweet Tahini Dressing:
- 1 Garlic Clove (Minced)
- 3 Tbsp Nutritional Yeast
- ¼ Cup Tahini
- ¼ Cup Water (Plus More As Needed To Thin)
- Salt/Pepper to Taste
- 3 Tbsp Balsamic Vinegar
- 2 Tbsp Pure Maple Syrup

Directions:
1. Preheat the oven to 400 degrees Fahrenheit.
2. Follow the package directions for cooking the rice.
3. Arrange cauliflower and broccoli on a baking pan together. On a separate baking sheet, spread chickpeas and carrots. Toss the vegetables with 1 tsp oil on each baking sheet. Season to taste with salt and pepper.
4. Roast for 20-30 minutes, turning the pans every ten minutes and shaking them. Cauliflower and broccoli require 30 minutes to cook, while carrots and chickpeas take 20 minutes, so start with the broccoli/cauliflower and add the chickpeas/carrots after the first 10 minutes. (Because every oven is different, keep an eye on them to make sure they do not burn.)
5. In a small bowl or cup, mix together all of the dressing ingredients until smooth. To thin, add more water as needed. Remove from the equation.
6. As soon as the vegetables and chickpeas are done, assemble your bowls! In each bowl, combine rice, broccoli, cauliflower, carrots, chickpeas, sesame seeds, and dressing.

Per serving: Calories: 540 Kcal; Fat: 16 g; Carbs: 84 g; Protein: 25 g: Sodium: 580 mg

84. Creamy Cauliflower Chickpea Curry

Preparation time: 15 minutes
Cooking time: 20 minutes
Servings: 4
Ingredients:
- 2-3 Tbsp fresh chopped cilantro
- Salt and pepper to taste.
- Rice, bread, cauliflower or rice for serving
- 2 Tbsp coconut oil
- 1 Medium white onion diced
- 3-4 Garlic cloves minced
- 1 Small cauliflower head chopped into small florets
- 1 Can chickpeas 15 oz., drained and rinsed
- 1 Can diced tomatoes 15 oz.
- 1 Can coconut milk 14 oz.
- 1-Inch fresh ginger peeled and grated
- 2 Tbsp red curry paste
- 1 Large red bell pepper diced

Directions:
1. Melt the coconut oil and onion in a large skillet over medium-high heat.
2. Add garlic, ginger, red curry paste, and bell pepper after 3-4 minutes of sautéing. Cook, stirring occasionally, for another 2 to 3 minutes.
3. Combine the remaining ingredients: cauliflower florets, chickpeas, diced tomatoes, coconut milk, salt, and pepper in a mixing bowl.
4. Reduce to a low heat and continue to cook for 10-12 minutes or until the cauliflower is fork-tender and the sauce thickens.
5. Season with salt and pepper to taste. Serve the curry in bowls with fresh cilantro on top. Enjoy while it is hot.

Per serving: Calories: 415 Kcal; Fat: 25 g; Carbs: 32 g; Protein: 11 g: Sodium: 490 mg

85. Stuffed Portobello Mushrooms with Spinach

Preparation time: 15 minutes
Cooking time: 25 minutes
Servings: 3
Ingredients:

- 4 Large sized Portobello mushroom stems, caps, and gills removed
- ¼ Cup chopped pepperoni
- ¼ Cup grated parmesan cheese
- ¼ Cup shredded mozzarella cheese, divided
- 1 Tablespoon reduced-fat Italian salad dressing
- 3 Tablespoons seasoned bread crumbs, divided
- 1 Clove garlic, minced
- Salt and ground black pepper to taste
- 1 (10 Ounce) bag fresh spinach, chopped
- 1 Egg

Directions:

1. Preheat the oven to 350 degrees Fahrenheit (175 degrees C).
2. Spread Italian dressing on both sides of each Portobello mushroom cap. Place the mushroom on a baking sheet with the gills facing up.
3. Bake mushrooms for 12 minutes in a preheated oven until soft. Drain any liquid that has accumulated in the mushrooms.
4. In a large mixing bowl, whisk together the egg, garlic, salt, and black pepper.
5. In a large mixing bowl, whisk together the eggs, spinach, pepperoni, Parmesan cheese, 3 tablespoons mozzarella cheese, and 3 tablespoons bread crumbs until well combined.
6. Sprinkle the remaining 1 tablespoon mozzarella cheese and 1 tablespoon bread crumbs on top of the spinach mixture in the mushroom caps. Place the mushrooms back in the oven.
7. Bake for another 15 minutes or until the topping is golden brown and the cheese has melted.

Per serving: Calories: 168 Kcal; Fat: 10 g; Carbs: 7 g; Protein: 11 g: Sodium: 590 mg

86. Veggie-Stuffed Portobello Mushrooms

Preparation time: 25 minutes
Cooking time: 15 minutes
Servings: 4
Ingredients:

- 4 Slices provolone cheese
- 1 Celery, thinly sliced
- 2 Cloves garlic, minced
- 2 – 3 Tablespoons olive oil
- 1 Tablespoon snipped fresh basil
- 1 Tablespoon lemon juice
- 1 Yellow sweet pepper, cut in bite-size strips
- 1 Small red onion, chopped
- 1 Medium zucchini, coarsely shredded
- 1 Carrot, coarsely shredded
- 4, 4 Inches portobello mushroom caps, stems removed
- 1 5-Ounce package fresh baby spinach
- ½ Cup fine dry bread crumbs
- ½ Cup finely shredded parmesan cheese

Directions:

1. Preheat the oven to 425 degrees Fahrenheit. Line a 15x10x1- inch baking tray with foil.
2. Cook and stir sweet pepper, onion, zucchini, carrot, celery, and garlic in heated oil for 4 minutes in a 12-inch skillet over medium-high heat.
3. Combine basil, parsley, lemon juice, 1/4 teaspoon salt, and ground black pepper in a large mixing bowl.
4. Cover with spinach and a lid.
5. Cook until the spinach has wilted, about 2 minutes.

6. Remove the pan from the heat. Set aside half of the Parmesan cheese and the crumbs from the spinach mixture.

7. If desired, remove the gills from the mushrooms.

8. Place the mushrooms, stems up, on the preheated pan. Place a piece of provolone cheese on top of each one.

9. Fill mushroom caps halfway with spinach mixture and cook 15 minutes in the oven (mushrooms will water out slightly).

10. The remaining Parmesan should be sprinkled on top. Cook 2 minutes more in the oven

Per serving: Calories: 290 Kcal; Fat: 17 g; Carbs: 24 g; Protein: 5 g: Sodium: 600 mg

87. Cauliflower Hash with Carrots

Preparation time: 10 minutes

Cooking time: 10 minutes

Servings: 4

Ingredients:
- 2 cups diced carrots
- 4 cups cauliflower florets
- ½ teaspoon ground cumin
- 3 tablespoons extra-virgin olive oil
- 1 tablespoon minced garlic
- 1 teaspoon salt
- 1 large onion, chopped

Directions:
1. Sauté for 1 minute with the onion and garlic. Stir in the carrots and cook for 3 minutes on high heat.
2. Toss the cauliflower florets with the cumin and salt to blend.
3. Cook for 3 minutes, or until gently browned, covered. Stir well and simmer for 3 to 4 minutes, uncovered, until softened.
4. Remove the pan from the heat and serve immediately.

Per serving: Calories: 160 Kcal; Fat: 10 g; Carbs: 14 g; Protein: 3 g: Sodium: 650 mg

88. Garlicky Zucchini Cubes with Mint

Preparation time: 5 minutes

Cooking time: 10 minutes

Servings: 4

Ingredients:
- 1 teaspoon salt
- 1 teaspoon dried mint
- 3 large green zucchini, cut into ½-inch cubes
- 3 tablespoons extra-virgin olive oil
- 1 large onion, chopped
- 3 cloves garlic, minced

Directions:
1. In a large skillet, heat the olive oil over medium heat.
2. Add the onion and garlic and cook, stirring constantly, for 3 minutes, or until softened.
3. Cook for 5 minutes, or until the zucchini is browned and soft, after adding the zucchini cubes and salt.
4. Toss the mint into the skillet to mix, and then cook for another 2 minutes.
5. Warm the dish before serving.

Per serving: Calories: 145 Kcal; Fat: 10 g; Carbs: 11 g; Protein: 4.3 g: Sodium: 602 mg

89. Zucchini and Artichokes Bowl with Farro

Preparation time: 15 minutes

Cooking time: 10 minutes

Servings: 4-6

Ingredients:
- 3 cups cooked farro
- Salt and freshly ground black pepper, to taste
- $^1/_3$ cup extra-virgin olive oil
- $^1/_3$ cup red onions, chopped
- ½ cup chopped red bell pepper

- ½ cup canned chickpeas, drained and rinsed
- ½ cup crumbled feta cheese, for serving (optional)
- ¼ cup sliced olives, for serving (optional)
- 3 tablespoons balsamic vinegar, for serving (optional)
- 2 garlic cloves, minced
- 1 cup zucchini, cut into ½-inch-thick slices
- ½ cup coarsely chopped artichokes
- 2 tablespoons fresh basil, chiffonade, for serving (optional)

Directions:

1. In a large skillet, heat the olive oil over medium heat until it shimmers.
2. Add the onions, bell pepper, and garlic and cook, stirring occasionally, for 5 minutes, or until softened.
3. Sauté for about 5 minutes, until the zucchini slices, artichokes, and chickpeas are somewhat soft.
4. Toss in the cooked farro until it is thoroughly heated. Season with salt and pepper to taste.
5. The mixture should be divided into bowls. Sprinkle the feta cheese, olive slices, and basil evenly over each bowl, then drizzle with balsamic vinegar if preferred.

Per serving: Calories: 361 Kcal; Fat: 20 g; Carbs: 50 g; Protein: 9 g: Sodium: 85 mg

90. Zucchini Fritters

Preparation time: 15 minutes

Cooking time: 5 minutes

Servings: 14 fritters (7 persons)

Ingredients:

- ⅛ teaspoon black pepper
- 2 tablespoons olive oil
- 4 cups grated zucchini
- Salt, to taste
- 2 large eggs, lightly beaten
- ⅔ all-purpose flour
- ⅓ cup scallions, sliced (green and white parts)

Directions:

1. In a colander, shred the zucchini and season liberally with salt. Allow 10 minutes for resting. Squeeze out as much liquid as you can from the shredded zucchini.
2. In a mixing bowl, grate the zucchini. In a large mixing bowl, whisk together the beaten eggs, scallions, flour, salt, and pepper until thoroughly mixed.
3. In a large skillet, heat the olive oil over medium heat until it is hot.
4. To make each fritter, drop 3 teaspoons of the zucchini mixture onto the hot skillet, flattening lightly into rounds and spacing them approximately 2 inches apart.
5. Cook for a total of 2 to 3 minutes. Cook for another 2 minutes, or until the zucchini fritters are golden brown and properly cooked.
6. Transfer to a dish lined with paper towels after removing from the heat. Continue with the rest of the zucchini mixture.
7. Serve immediately.

Per serving: Calories: 113 Kcal; Fat: 6 g; Carbs: 12 g; Protein: 4 g: Sodium: 25 mg

91. Moroccan Tagine with Vegetables

Preparation time: 20 minutes

Cooking time: 40 minutes

Servings: 2

Ingredients: '

- 2 tablespoons olive oil
- ½ onion, diced
- 1 garlic clove, minced
- 2 cups cauliflower florets
- 1 medium carrot, cut into 1-inch pieces
- 1 cup diced eggplant

- 1 (28-ounce / 794-g) can whole tomatoes with their juices
- 1 (15-ounce / 425-g) can chickpeas, drained and rinsed
- 2 small red potatoes, cut into 1-inch pieces
- 1 cup water
- 1 teaspoon pure maple syrup
- ½ teaspoon salt
- 1 to 2 teaspoons harissa paste

Directions:

1. Heat the olive oil in a Dutch oven over medium-high heat. Cook, stirring periodically, for 5 minutes, or until the onion is transparent.
2. Garlic, cauliflower florets, carrot, eggplant, tomatoes, and potatoes should all be added at this point. Break up the tomatoes into smaller pieces using a wooden spoon or spatula.
3. Stir together the chickpeas, water, maple syrup, cinnamon, turmeric, cumin, and salt. Bring the pot of water to a boil.
4. Reduce the heat to medium-low once it begins to boil. Stir in the harissa paste, cover, and cook for 40 minutes, or until the veggies are tender. Then season to taste and make any necessary adjustments.
5. Allow the mixture to cool for 5 minutes before serving.

Per serving: Calories: 298 Kcal; Fat: 10 g; Carbs: 45 g; Protein: 11 g: Sodium: 335 mg

92. Acorn squash with Apples

Preparation time: 15 minutes
Cooking time: 10 minutes
Servings: 2
Ingredients:

- 1 small sized acorn squash, almost 6 inches in diameter
- 2 teaspoons trans-fat-free margarine
- 1 green apple, peeled, cored and sliced
- 2 tbsps. brown sugar

Directions:

1. Combine the apple and brown sugar in a small bowl. Remove from the equation.
2. Using a sharp knife, pierce the squash many times to allow steam to escape during cooking. Microwave on high for 5 minutes, or until tender. After 3 minutes, turn the squash to achieve equal cooking.
3. Slice the squash in half on a cutting board. Remove the seeds from the center of each half and toss them out. Fill the squash with the apple mixture that has been hollowed out.
4. Return the squash to the microwave and cook for another 2 minutes, or until the apples are softened.
5. Place the squash on a serving platter. Serve immediately with 1 teaspoon margarine on each half.

Per serving: Calories: 205 Kcal; Fat: 4 g; Carbs: 35 g; Protein: 2 g: Sodium: 46 mg

93. Asparagus with Hazelnut Gremolata

Preparation time: 15 minutes
Cooking time: 5-10 minutes
Servings: 8
Ingredients:

- 4 teaspoons fresh lemon juice
- 2 teaspoons extra-virgin olive oil
- 2 pounds asparagus, tough ends removed, then peeled if skin is thick
- 2 cloves garlic, minced
- 2 tablespoons finely chopped toasted hazelnuts (filberts)
- 1/2 teaspoon grated lemon zest, some extra for garnish
- 1/2 teaspoon salt
- 2 tablespoons chopped fresh flat-leaf (Italian) parsley, plus sprigs for garnish

Directions:

1. Bring 4 cups of water to a boil in a big saucepan with a steamer basket. Then add the asparagus, cover it with a lid, and steam for 4 minutes, or until tender-crisp. Remove the pot from the heat.
2. Toss the asparagus, garlic, chopped parsley, hazelnuts, 1/4 teaspoon lemon zest, lemon juice, olive oil, and salt together in a large mixing dish. Toss to combine and coat.
3. Arrange the asparagus on a serving plate and top with lemon zest and parsley sprigs. Serve right away.

Per serving: Calories: 50 Kcal; Fat: 2 g; Carbs: 5 g; Protein: 3 g: Sodium: 150 mg

94. Baked Apples with Cherries and Almonds

Preparation time: 20 minutes
Cooking time: 1 hour
Servings: 6
Ingredients:
- 2 tablespoons dark honey
- 2 teaspoons walnut oil or canola oil
- 1/3 cup dried cherries, coarsely chopped
- 3 tablespoons chopped almonds
- 1 tablespoon wheat germ
- /4 pounds total weight
- 1/2 cup apple juice
- 1/4 cup water
-

Directions:
1. First, preheat the oven to 350 degrees Fahrenheit (180 degrees Celsius).
2. Toss the cherries, almonds, wheat germ, brown sugar, cinnamon, and nutmeg together in a small mixing basin until well combined. Remove the item from circulation. If you prefer, you can leave the apples peeled.

3. Peel each apple in a circular motion, skipping every other row so that rows of peel alternate with rows of apple flesh, using a vegetable peeler or a sharp knife.
4. Core each apple beginning at the stem end and ending 3/4 inch from the bottom. Evenly distribute the cherry mixture among the apples, gently pressing the mixture into each cavity.
5. Arrange the apples in an ovenproof frying pan or a small baking dish large enough to hold them upright. Fill the pan with apple juice and water.
6. Cover the pan tightly with aluminum foil and drizzle the honey and oil equally over the apples.
7. Bake for 50 to 60 minutes, or until the apples are soft when pricked with a knife.
8. Drizzle the pan juices over the apples and place them on individual plates. Serve warm or at room temperature.

Per serving: Calories: 200 Kcal; Fat: 4 g; Carbs: 35 g; Protein: 2 g: Sodium: 7 mg

95. Braised Celery Root

Preparation time: 15 minutes
Cooking time: 20 minutes
Servings: 6
Ingredients:
- 1 cup vegetable stock or broth
- 1 celery root (celeriac), peeled and diced (about 3 cups)
- 1/4 cup sour cream
- 1 teaspoon dijon mustard
- 1/4 teaspoon salt
- 1/4 teaspoon freshly ground black pepper
- 2 teaspoons fresh thyme leaves

Directions:
1. Bring the stock to a boil in a large saucepan over high heat. Add the celery

root and mix well. Reduce the heat to low when the stock returns to a boil.

2. Cover and cook, turning occasionally, for 10 to 12 minutes, or until the celery root is soft.

3. Transfer the celery root to a bowl with a slotted spoon; cover and keep it warm. Raise the heat to high and bring the cooking liquid to a boil in the saucepan.

4. Cook, uncovered, for 5 minutes or until the liquid has been reduced to 1 tablespoon.

5. Whisk in the sour cream, mustard, salt, and pepper after removing the pan from the heat. Stir in the celery root and thyme until the sauce is well cooked over medium heat.

6. Serve immediately in a hot serving dish.

Per serving: Calories: 55 Kcal; Fat: 2 g; Carbs: 7 g; Protein: 2 g: Sodium: 205 mg

96. Braised Kale with Cherry Tomatoes

Preparation time: 15 minutes

Cooking time: 15-20 minutes

Servings: 6

Ingredients:

- 1 tablespoon fresh lemon juice
- 1/4 teaspoon salt
- 2 teaspoons extra-virgin olive oil
- 4 garlic cloves, thinly sliced
- 1 cup cherry tomatoes, halved
- 1/8 teaspoon freshly ground black pepper
- 1 pound kale, (remove the tough stems and chop leaves)
- 1/2 cup of low-sodium vegetable stock/broth

Directions:

1. Heat the olive oil in a large frying pan over medium heat. Add garlic and sauté for about 1 or 2 minutes until slightly brown.

2. Combine the kale and vegetable stock in a mixing bowl and cover it. Reduce

decrease the heat to medium-low, and cook for about 5 minutes, or until the kale has wilted and part of the liquid has evaporated.

3. Cook, stirring occasionally, until the kale is soft, about 5 to 7 minutes longer. Remove the pan from the heat and add the lemon juice, salt, and pepper to taste. You can serve it immediately.

Per serving: Calories: 70 Kcal; Fat: 2 g; Carbs: 9 g; Protein: 4 g: Sodium: 133 mg

97. Baby Minted Carrots

Preparation time: 5 minutes

Cooking time: 15 minutes

Servings: 6

Ingredients:

- 1/2 tablespoon chopped fresh mint leaves
- 1/8 teaspoon ground cinnamon
- 6 cups water
- 1 pound baby carrots, rinsed (about 5 1/2 cups)
- 1 tablespoon cornstarch
- 1/4 cup 100% apple juice

Directions:

1. Place the carrots and fill halfway with water. Boil for 10 minutes, or until the carrots are tender-crisp. Drain and place the carrots in a serving bowl.

2. Combine the apple juice and cornstarch in a small saucepan over medium heat. Stir for 5 minutes, or until the mixture thickens. Combine the mint and cinnamon in a mixing bowl.

3. Over the carrots, pour the mixture. Serve right away.

Per serving: Calories: 45 Kcal; Fat: 0 g; Carbs: 10 g; Protein: 1 g: Sodium: 50 mg

98. Broccoli with Garlic and Lemon

Preparation time: 10 minutes

Cooking time: 10 minutes

Servings: 4

Ingredients:

- 1/4 teaspoon kosher salt
- 1/4 teaspoon ground black pepper
- 4 cups broccoli florets
- 1 teaspoon lemon zest
- 1 teaspoon olive oil
- 1 tablespoon minced garlic

Directions:

1. Boil 1 cup of water and cook broccoli for 2 to 3 minutes, or until the broccoli is tender. Drain the broccoli and set it aside.
2. Heat the oil in a small sauté pan over medium-high heat. Sauté for 30 seconds after adding the garlic. Combine the broccoli, lemon zest, salt, and pepper in a large mixing bowl. Toss everything together and serve.

Per serving: Calories: 45 Kcal; Fat: g; 1 Carbs: 7 g; Protein: 3 g: Sodium: 150 mg

99. Cauliflower Mashed 'Potatoes'

Preparation time: 20 minutes

Cooking time: 20-30 minutes

Servings: 4

Ingredients:

- 1 head cauliflower
- 1 clove garlic
- Pepper to taste
- 1 leek, white only, cut in 4 pieces
- 1 teaspoon butter
- 2 teaspoons olive oil

Directions:

1. Cauliflower should be broken into small pieces. Steam cauliflower, garlic, and leeks in water in a large saucepan until thoroughly soft, about 20 to 30 minutes.
2. Puree the vegetables in a food processor until they resemble mashed potatoes. Only process a limited amount at a time.
3. Use a blender if you want a smoother texture. Use a dish towel to firmly hold the blender lid in place. If the vegetables appear to be dry, add a splash of boiling water.
4. Add the butter and olive oil and mix well. Season with salt and pepper to taste. Serve.

Per serving: Calories: 80 Kcal; Fat: 4 g; Carbs: 11 g; Protein: 3 g: Sodium: 55 mg

100. Cheesy Baked Zucchini

Preparation time: 20 minutes

Cooking time: 30-35 minutes

Servings: 2

Ingredients:

- 1/8 teaspoon onion powder
- 2 tablespoons grated Parmesan cheese
- 1 medium zucchini, about 6 inches long
- 1 teaspoon olive oil
- 1/8 teaspoon garlic powder

Directions:

1. Preheat the oven to 375 degrees Fahrenheit. Remove the zucchini's ends. Slice the zucchini most of the way through at every half-inch down the length, but not all the way down.
2. Although the zucchini should appear to be sliced in rounds, all of the slices are still attached underneath.
3. Using a paper towel, gently blot the zucchini dry. Place the zucchini on a big sheet of foil large enough to wrap around it entirely.
4. Drizzle olive oil over the zucchini's top. Garlic and onion powders are sprinkled on top.
5. Wrap the zucchini with foil and secure it with a pinch. Place it on a baking pan to cool.

6. Preheat the oven to 350°F and bake for 30–35 minutes, or until the zucchini is soft when pierced with a fork. Remove the foil from the oven and remove it. Using a fork, smear the cheese over the zucchini. The foil should be left open.

7. Return the zucchini to the oven for 1 to 2 minutes, or until the cheese has melted and begun to color. Warm the dish before serving.

Per serving: Calories: 64 Kcal; Fat: 4 g; Carbs: 4 g; Protein: 3 g: Sodium: 85 mg

Chapter 6: Vegan Recipes

101. Grilled Vegetable Sewers

Preparation time: 15 minutes

Cooking time: 10 minutes

Servings: 4

Ingredients:

- 4 medium red onions, peel and slice into 6 wedges
- 2 beefsteak tomatoes, cut into quarters
- 4 red bell peppers, cut into 2-inch squares
- 4 medium zucchini, cut into slices
- 2 yellow bell peppers, cut into squares
- 2 orange bell peppers, cut into squares
- 2 tablespoons & 1 teaspoon olive oil
- Special Equipment:
- 4 wooden skewers, soaked in water for at least 30 minutes

Directions:

1. Preheat your grill to medium-high.
2. Alternate between red onion, zucchini, tomatoes, and the other colored bell peppers on the skewers. 2 tablespoons olive oil, brushed on them
3. Grill the vegetable skewers for 5 minutes after brushing the grill grates with 1 teaspoon of olive oil. Grill for another 5 minutes, or until the skewers are cooked to your taste.
4. Allow 5 minutes for the skewers to cool before serving.

Per serving: Calories: 115 Kcal; Fat: 3 g; Carbs: 18.7 g; Protein: 3.5 g: Sodium: 12 mg; Sugar: 4.7 g

102. Honey Sage Carrots

Preparation time: 15 minutes

Cooking time: 15 minutes

Servings: 4

Ingredients:

- 1 tablespoon chopped fresh sage
- 2 cups sliced carrots
- 2 teaspoons butter
- 1/4 teaspoon ground black pepper
- 1/8 teaspoon salt
- 2 tablespoons honey

Directions:

1. Bring a medium saucepan of water to a rolling boil.
2. Boil for 5 minutes, or until carrots are, fork tender.
3. Drain the water and set it aside.
4. Add butter to a medium sauté pan and heat it up.
5. Once the butter has melted and the pan is heated, add the carrots, honey, sage, pepper, and salt. Cook, stirring regularly, for about 3 minutes.
6. Remove the pan from the heat and serve.

Per serving: Calories: 74 Kcal; Fat: 1 g; Carbs: 15 g; Protein: 1 g: Sodium: 12 mg; Sugar: 12 g

103. Wilted Dandelion Greens with Sweet Onion

Preparation time: 15 minutes

Cooking time: 15 minutes

Servings: 4

Ingredients:

- ½ cup low-sodium vegetable broth
- 1 tablespoon extra-virgin olive oil
- 2 bunches dandelion greens, roughly chopped
- Freshly ground black pepper, to taste
- 2 garlic cloves, minced
- 1 Vidalia onion, thinly sliced

Directions:

1. In a large skillet, heat the olive oil over low heat.
2. Add the garlic and onion and simmer, turning occasionally, for 2 to 3 minutes, or until the onion is transparent.
3. Stir in the vegetable broth and dandelion greens and cook, stirring regularly, for 5 to 7 minutes, or until wilted.
4. Season with black pepper and serve immediately on a platter

Per serving: Calories: 81 Kcal; Fat: 3.9 g; Carbs: 10 g; Protein: 3.2 g: Sodium: 72 mg; Sugar: 3.1 g

104.   Lentil Ragout

Preparation time: 40 minutes

Cooking time: 25 minutes

Servings: 6

Ingredients:

- 1 teaspoon kosher salt
- 1/4 teaspoon ground black pepper
- 1 teaspoon olive oil
- 1 cup chopped onions
- 5 cups water
- 1 cup raw red lentils
- 1 tablespoon chopped fresh thyme
- 6 medium tomatoes, chopped
- 4 cloves garlic, minced

Directions:

1. In a medium saucepan, heat the oil over medium-high heat.
2. Add onions into the oil. For 2 to 3 minutes, sauté the onions.
3. Add the tomatoes and cook for 3 minutes more, stirring constantly.
4. Cook, stirring occasionally, until the lentils have absorbed the majority of the liquid, about 20 minutes.
5. Add the thyme, garlic, salt, and pepper to taste. Ragout should have a thick consistency but not be dry.

Per serving: Calories: 152 Kcal; Fat: 1 g; Carbs: 27 g; Protein: 10 g: Sodium: 179 mg; Sugar: 5 g

105.   Celery and Mustard Greens

Preparation time: 10 minutes

Cooking time: 15 minutes

Servings: 4

Ingredients:

- 1 bunch mustard greens, roughly chopped
- ½ cup low-sodium vegetable broth
- ½ large red bell pepper, thinly sliced
- 2 garlic cloves, minced
- 1 celery stalk, roughly chopped
- ½ sweet onion, chopped

Directions:

1. In a large cast iron pan, bring the vegetable broth to a simmer over medium heat.
2. Combine the celery, onion, bell pepper, and garlic in a mixing bowl. Cook for 3 to 5 minutes, uncovered, or until the onion is softened.
3. Toss in the mustard greens and toss thoroughly. Cook for an additional 10 minutes, covered, on low heat, or until the liquid has evaporated and the greens have wilted.
4. Remove the pan from the heat and serve immediately.

Per serving: Calories: 39 Kcal; Fat: 0 g; Carbs: 3.1 g; Protein: 3.1 g: Sodium: 120 mg; Sugar: 0.7 g

106.   Potato Salad

Preparation time: 30 minutes

Cooking time: 0 minutes

Servings: 4

Ingredients:

- 1/2 teaspoon ground black pepper
- 1/2 pound potatoes, diced and boiled or steamed

- 1/2 large yellow onion, chopped (1 cup)
- 1/8 cup low-calorie mayonnaise
- 1/2 large carrot, diced (1/2 cup)
- 1 ribs celery, diced (1/2 cup)
- 1/2 tablespoon Dijon mustard
- 1 tablespoon red wine vinegar
- 1 tablespoon minced fresh dill (or 1/2 tablespoon dried)

Directions:
1. In a mixing bowl, combine all of the ingredients and combine.
2. Before serving, chill the dish.

Per serving: Calories: 77 Kcal; Fat: 1 g; Carbs: 14 g; Protein: 1 g: Sodium: 127 mg; Sugar: 0 g

107. Vegetable and Tofu Scramble

Preparation time: 5 minutes
Cooking time: 10 minutes
Servings: 2
Ingredients:
- 2 garlic cloves, minced
- Pinch red pepper flakes
- 2 tablespoons extra-virgin olive oil
- ½ red onion, finely chopped
- 1 cup chopped kale
- 8 ounces tofu, cut into pieces
- ½ teaspoon sea salt
- 8 ounces mushrooms, sliced
- ⅛ teaspoon freshly ground black pepper

Directions:
1. In a medium nonstick skillet, heat the olive oil over medium-high heat until it shimmers.
2. Cook, turning periodically, for about 5 minutes, or until the onions, kale, and mushrooms begin to brown in the skillet.
3. Stir in the tofu for 3 to 4 minutes, or until softened.

4. Cook for 30 seconds after adding the garlic, red pepper flakes, salt, and black pepper.
5. Allow 5 minutes for the mixture to cool before serving.

Per serving: Calories: 233 Kcal; Fat: 15.9 g; Carbs: 11.9 g; Protein: 13.4 g: Sodium: 672 mg; Sugar: 7.7 g

108. Chinese Style Asparagus

Preparation time: 20 minutes
Cooking time: 5 minutes
Servings: 6
Ingredients:
- 1 teaspoon reduced-sodium soy sauce
- 1/2 cup water
- 1/2 teaspoon sugar
- 1 1/2 pounds fresh asparagus, remove woody ends and cut into 1 ½ inch lengths

Directions:
1. Heat the water, sugar, and soy sauce in a large saucepan over high heat.
2. Cook until the water is boiling, then add the asparagus.
3. Reduce the heat to low and cook for 3 to 4 minutes, or until the asparagus is tender-crisp.
4. Immediately transfer to a serving plate and serve.

Per serving: Calories: 24 Kcal; Fat: 0 g; Carbs: 4 g; Protein: 2 g: Sodium: 26 mg; Sugar: 0 g

109. Zoodles

Preparation time: 10 minutes
Cooking time: 5 minutes
Servings: 2
Ingredients:
- 2 tablespoons avocado oil
- 2 medium zucchini, spiralized
- ¼ teaspoon salt, or to your taste
- Freshly ground black pepper, to taste

Directions:

1. In a large skillet, heat the avocado oil over medium heat until it shimmers.
2. Toss the zucchini noodles with the salt and black pepper in the skillet to coat. Cook, stirring regularly, for 1 to 2 minutes, or until the vegetables are soft.
3. Warm the dish before serving.

Per serving: Calories: 128 Kcal; Fat: 14 g; Carbs: 0.3 g; Protein: 0.3 g: Sodium: 291 mg; Sugar: 5 g

110. Creole Style Black Eyed Peas

Preparation time: 20 minutes

Cooking time: 2 hours

Servings: 8

Ingredients:

- 1/4 teaspoon cayenne pepper
- 1 bay leaf
- 2 stalks celery, finely chopped
- 3 teaspoons minced garlic
- 3 cups water
- 2 cups dried black-eyed peas
- 2 cups canned unsalted tomatoes, crushed
- 1 large onion, finely chopped
- 1/2 teaspoon dry mustard
- 1/4 teaspoon ground ginger
- 1/2 cup chopped parsley
- 1 teaspoon low-sodium vegetable-flavored bouillon granules

Directions:

1. 2 cups water and black-eyed peas in a medium saucepan over high heat.
2. Bring to a boil for 2 minutes, then cover and set aside to cool for 1 hour.
3. Remove the peas from the pot and drain the water.
4. Add the remaining 1 cup of water, the bouillon granules, the tomatoes, onion, celery, garlic, mustard, ginger, cayenne pepper, and bay leaf, along with the remaining 1 cup of water.

5. Bring to a boil, stirring constantly.
6. Cover, turn down the heat, and cook for 2 hours, stirring regularly. As needed, add water to keep the peas submerged in liquid.
7. Remove the bay leaf and place the soup in a serving bowl with parsley on top. Serve right away.

Per serving: Calories: 168 Kcal; Fat: 1 g; Carbs: 31 g; Protein: 11 g: Sodium: 50 mg; Sugar: 0 g

111. Sweet Pepper Stew

Preparation time: 20 minutes

Cooking time: 50 minutes

Servings: 2

Ingredients:

- 1 cup low-sodium vegetable stock
- 2 tablespoons olive oil
- 2 sweet peppers, diced (about 2 cups)
- ½ large onion, minced
- 1 tablespoon gluten-free Worcestershire sauce
- 1 garlic clove, minced
- ¼ cup brown rice
- ¼ cup brown lentils
- 1 teaspoon oregano
- 1 cup low-sodium tomato juice
- Salt, to taste

Directions:

1. Heat the olive oil in a Dutch oven over medium-high heat.
2. Sauté the sweet peppers and onion for 10 minutes or until the onion becomes golden and the peppers are wilted, turning periodically.
3. Cook for another 30 seconds after adding the garlic, Worcestershire sauce, and oregano.
4. Stir together the tomato juice, vegetable stock, rice, and lentils in the Dutch oven.
5. Bring the mixture to a boil, and then decrease to a medium-low heat setting. Cover and cook for 45 minutes, or until

the rice is soft and the lentils are cooked through.

6. Season with salt and serve immediately.

Per serving: Calories: 378 Kcal; Fat: 11 g; Carbs: 52 g; Protein: 11 g: Sodium: 391 mg; Sugar: 6.3 g

112. Eggplant with Toasted Spices

Preparation time: 15 minutes
Cooking time: 10 minutes
Servings: 6
Ingredients:

- 1 tablespoon light molasses
- Pinch of ground cloves
- 1/4 teaspoon freshly ground black pepper
- 1 tablespoon chopped fresh cilantro
- 1 large eggplant, about 1 1/2 pounds
- 1 teaspoon mustard seed
- 1/2 teaspoon ground cumin
- 1/2 teaspoon ground coriander
- 1/2 teaspoon curry powder
- 1 tablespoon olive oil
- 1/2 yellow onion, finely chopped
- 2 cups cherry tomatoes, halved, or 1 cup tomato sauce
- 1 teaspoon red wine vinegar
- 1 garlic clove, minced
- Pinch of ground ginger
- Pinch of ground nutmeg
- 1/4 teaspoon salt

Directions:

1. In a charcoal grill, build a hot fire, or heat a gas grill or broiler.
2. Spray the rack or broiler pan gently with cooking spray away from the heat source.
3. 4 to 6 inches away from the heat source, place the cooking rack.
4. Trim the eggplant and slice it into 1/4-inch thick circular slices.
5. Arrange the slices on the rack or pan and grill or broil, rotating once, for

about 5 minutes on each side, until the eggplant is soft and browned.

6. Remove from the oven and keep warm.
7. Combine the first seven spices in a small bowl.
8. Heat the olive oil in a large frying pan over medium heat until it is hot but not smoking.
9. Cook, stirring constantly, for about 30 seconds after adding the spice combination.
10. Add the onion and cook for 4 minutes, or until tender and transparent.
11. Combine the tomatoes, molasses, garlic, and vinegar in a mixing bowl. Cook, stirring periodically, until the sauce has thickened, about 4 minutes. Season with salt and pepper to taste.
12. Pour the sauce over the eggplant in a hot serving dish or individual plates, and top with the cilantro.

Per serving: Calories: 128 Kcal; Fat: 4 g; Carbs: 20 g; Protein: 3 g: Sodium: 160 mg; Sugar: 0 g

113. Vegetable and Red Lentil Stew

Preparation time: 10 minutes
Cooking time: 35 minutes
Servings: 6
Ingredients:

- 4 celery stalks, finely diced
- 1 tablespoon extra-virgin olive oil
- 6½ cups water
- 1 teaspoon salt, plus more as needed
- 2 zucchini, finely diced
- 3 cups red lentils
- 1 teaspoon dried oregano
- 2 onions, peeled and finely diced

Directions:

1. In a large pot over medium heat, heat the olive oil.
2. Add the onions and cook, stirring constantly, for about 5 minutes, or until they are softened.

3. Bring the water, zucchini, celery, lentils, oregano, and salt to a boil in a large pot.
4. Reduce the heat to low and cover for 30 minutes, or until the lentils are cooked, stirring occasionally.
5. Season to taste and make any necessary adjustments.

Per serving: Calories: 387 Kcal; Fat: 4.4 g; Carbs: 63.7 g; Protein: 24 g: Sodium: 418 mg; Sugar: 4 g

114. Glazed Root Vegetable

Preparation time: 10 minutes
Cooking time: 1 hour
Servings: 4
Ingredients:
- 1 1/2 cups water
- 1/2 cup onions, cut into 1-inch pieces
- 2 teaspoons sugar
- 1/2 cup carrots, cut into 1-inch pieces
- 1 teaspoon olive oil
- 1/2 cup turnips, cut into 1-inch pieces
- 1/2 cup new potatoes, cut into 1-inch pieces

Directions:
1. Combine the water, onions, carrots, turnips, and potatoes in a saucepan.
2. Cook, uncovered, for 15 minutes over medium heat until vegetables are soft.
3. Drain and drizzle with olive oil and sugar.
4. Increase the heat to high and continue to cook, shaking the pan occasionally, until the veggies are coated, and brown.
5. Immediately transfer to a serving plate and serve.

Per serving: Calories: 57 Kcal; Fat: 1 g; Carbs: 10 g; Protein: 2 g: Sodium: 24 mg; Sugar: 2 g

115. Cauliflower Steaks with Arugula

Preparation time: 5 minutes
Cooking time: 20 minutes

Servings: 4
Ingredients:
- 1 head cauliflower
- 4 cups arugula
- Cooking spray
- ½ teaspoon garlic powder

Dressing:
- 1½ tablespoons honey mustard
- 1½ tablespoons extra-virgin olive oil
- 1 teaspoon freshly squeezed lemon juice

Directions:
1. Preheat the oven to 425 degrees Fahrenheit (220 degrees Celsius).
2. Cut the cauliflower head in half lengthwise after removing the leaves. Each portion should yield 112-inch-thick steaks.
3. Spray both sides of each steak with cooking spray and season with garlic powder on both sides.
4. Place the cauliflower steaks on a baking sheet and roast for 10 minutes, covered in foil.
5. To avoid steam, remove the baking sheet from the oven and gently draw back the foil. Cook for another 10 minutes uncovered after flipping the steaks.
6. In the meantime, prepare the dressing: In a small bowl, combine the olive oil, honey mustard, and lemon juice.
7. Divide the cauliflower steaks into four equal halves once thoroughly cooked. One-quarter of the arugula and dressing should go on top of each portion.
8. Serve right away.

Per serving: Calories: 115 Kcal; Fat: 6 g; Carbs: 14 g; Protein: 5 g: Sodium: 97 mg; Sugar: 13 g

116. Green Beans with Red Pepper and Garlic

Preparation time: 10 minutes

Cooking time: 10 minutes

Servings: 3

Ingredients:

- 1/2 teaspoon sesame oil
- 1/8 teaspoon salt
- 1/2 pound green beans, stems trimmed
- 1/2 red bell pepper, seeded and cut into thin slices
- 1 teaspoon olive oil
- 1/2 clove garlic, finely chopped
- 1/8 teaspoon freshly ground black pepper
- 1/4 teaspoon chili paste or red pepper flakes

Directions:

1. The beans should be cut into 2-inch chunks.
2. Bring a big saucepan of water to a boil, 3/4 full.
3. Cook for 1 to 3 minutes, or until the beans turn brilliant green and are tender-crisp.
4. To stop the cooking, drain the beans and place them in a dish of ice water.
5. Drain and set aside once more.
6. Heat the olive oil in a large frying pan over medium heat.
7. Toss and mix in the bell pepper for about 1 minute. Add the beans and cook for a further minute. Stir in the chili paste and garlic for 1 minute.
8. Tender and vivid green beans will be the result.

Per serving: Calories: 54 Kcal; Fat: 2 g; Carbs: 7 g; Protein: 2 g: Sodium: 103 mg; Sugar: 3 g

117. Grilled Romaine Lettuce

Preparation time: 5 minutes

Cooking time: 5 minutes

Servings: 4

Ingredients:

- 2 heads romaine lettuce, halved lengthwise
- 2 tablespoons extra-virgin olive oil

Dressing:

- ½ cup unsweetened almond milk
- 1 pinch red pepper flakes
- 1 tablespoon extra-virgin olive oil
- 1 garlic clove, pressed
- ¼ bunch fresh chives, thinly chopped

Directions:

1. Preheat a grill pan to medium-high heat.
2. Drizzle olive oil over each lettuce half. Place the lettuce halves on the grill, flat-side down. Grill the lettuce for 3 to 5 minutes or until it wilts slightly and gets mild grill marks.
3. In a small mixing bowl, whisk together all of the dressing ingredients.
4. Serve with 2 tablespoons of the dressing drizzled over each romaine half.

Per serving: Calories: 126 Kcal; Fat: 11 g; Carbs: 7 g; Protein: 2 g: Sodium: 41 mg; Sugar: 3 g

118. Brussels sprouts with Shallots and Lemon

Preparation time: 15 minutes

Cooking time: 15 minutes

Servings: 4

Ingredients:

- 1 tablespoon fresh lemon juice
- 3 teaspoons extra-virgin olive oil, divided
- 1 pound Brussels sprouts, trim and cut into quarters
- 3 shallots, thinly sliced (about 3 tablespoons)
- 1/4 teaspoon salt, divided
- 1/4 teaspoon finely grated lemon zest
- 1/4 teaspoon freshly ground black pepper
- 1/2 cup no-salt-added vegetable stock or broth

Directions:

1. Heat 2 teaspoons olive oil in a large nonstick frying pan over medium heat
2. Add the onions and cook for about 6 minutes, or until tender and faintly brown.
3. 1/8 teaspoon salt stirred in Place in a mixing dish and set aside.
4. Heat the remaining 1 teaspoon olive oil in the same frying pan over medium heat.
5. Sauté the Brussels sprouts for 3 to 4 minutes, or until they begin to color.
6. Bring the veggie stock to a low simmer.
7. Cook, uncovered, for 5 to 6 minutes, or until the Brussels sprouts are soft.
8. Toss the shallots back into the pan.
9. Add the lemon zest and juice, as well as the 1/8 teaspoon salt and pepper. Serve right away.

Per serving: Calories: 104 Kcal; Fat: 4 g; Carbs: 12 g; Protein: 5 g: Sodium: 191 mg; Sugar: 3 g

119. Chickpea Lettuce Wraps with Celery

Preparation time: 10 minutes

Cooking time: 0 minutes

Servings: 4

Ingredients:

- 2 tablespoons finely chopped red onion
- 3 tablespoons honey mustard
- 1 can low-sodium chickpeas, drained and rinsed
- 1 celery stalk, thinly sliced
- 1 tablespoon capers, undrained
- 12 butter lettuce leaves
- 2 tablespoons unsalted tahini

Directions:

1. Using a potato masher or the back of a fork, mash the chickpeas in a bowl until nearly smooth.

2. Stir in the celery, red onion, tahini, honey mustard, and capers until everything is well combined.
3. Place three overlapping lettuce leaves on a platter, top with a quarter of the mashed chickpea filling, and roll up for each serving.
4. Using the remaining lettuce leaves and chickpea mixture, repeat the process.

Per serving: Calories: 182Kcal; Fat: 7.1 g; Carbs: 19.6 g; Protein: 103 g: Sodium: 171 mg; Sugar: 12 g

120. Stir Fried Eggplant

Preparation time: 25 minutes

Cooking time: 15 minutes

Servings: 2

Ingredients:

- 1 cup water, plus more as needed
- 1 cup corn kernels
- 2 tablespoons almond butter
- 2 medium tomatoes, chopped
- 1 medium carrot, sliced
- 2 cups green beans, cut into 1-inch pieces
- 2 ribs celery, sliced
- ½ cup chopped red onion
- 1 tablespoon finely chopped garlic
- 1 small eggplant, peeled and cut into ½-inch cubes
- 1 tablespoon dried Italian herb seasoning
- 1 teaspoon ground cumin

Directions:

1. In a large soup pot, heat 1 tablespoon of water over medium-high heat until it sputters.
2. Cook for 2 minutes, adding a splash of water if necessary.
3. Stir-fry for 2 to 3 minutes with the garlic, Italian seasoning, cumin, and eggplant, adding a little more water as needed.

4. Stir in the carrots, green beans, celery, corn kernels, and ½ cup water. Reduce the heat to medium, cover, and simmer for 8 to 10 minutes, or until the veggies are soft, stirring occasionally.
5. In a separate bowl, combine the almond butter and ½ cup of water.
6. Stir in the almond butter mixture and chopped tomatoes after removing the veggies from the heat. Serve when it was cool.

Per serving: Calories: 176 Kcal; Fat: g; Carbs: 5.5 g; Protein: 5.8 g: Sodium: 198 mg;   Sugar: 8.7

Chapter 7: Fish and Seafood

121. Mediterranean Baked Fish

Preparation time: 30 minutes
Cooking time: 30 minutes
Servings: 4
Ingredients:

- 1 tablespoon olive oil
- 3 cloves garlic minced
- 4 oz. kalamata olives (or any of your choice)
- 1 tablespoon capers
- 28 oz. tomatoes canned crushed
- ¼ cup basil chopped fresh or 1 teaspoon dried
- 16 oz. white fish fillets
- 1 lemons sliced thinly
- salt and pepper to taste

Directions:

1. Preheat the oven to 190°C (375 degrees F)
2. Place your garlic in a frying pan with olive oil and cook until fragrant.
3. Toss in the smashed tomatoes, basil, and season to taste with salt and pepper (Mrs. Dash).
4. It would be ideal if you had a pan that you could take from stovetop to oven; an iron skillet is a little too rough for this meal, so it is a shame I had to dirty two pans.)
5. In an oven-safe dish or pan, place your fresh basil tomato sauce.
6. Place the fish on top of the tomato basil sauce. Top the fish fillets with thinly cut lemons. On top of the fish and tomatoes, scatter the drained olives and capers. If desired, pour a little olive oil on top before baking.
7. Bake your healthy Mediterranean fish for 15-25 minutes, uncovered, or until it flakes easily with a fork. (Oven time varies depending on the size and thickness of the fish.)
8. Enjoy with fresh basil as a garnish!

Per serving: Calories: 229 Kcal; Fat: 10 g; Carbs: 12 g; Protein: 25 g: Sodium: 566 mg; Sugar: 9.4 g

122. Sea Food Corn Chowder

Preparation time: 40 minutes
Cooking time: 25 minutes
Servings: 3
Ingredients:

- 4 ounces fresh or frozen skinless halibut fillets
- 2 fresh or frozen sea scallops (about 8 ounces total)
- 1/2 tablespoon canola oil
- 1/2 medium onion, chopped
- 1/2 medium green sweet pepper, seeded and chopped
- 1/2 clove garlic, minced
- 2 medium tomatoes, cored and coarsely chopped (about 3 cups)
- 1 cup lower-sodium vegetable broth
- 1/2 cup water
- 1/2 cup fresh or frozen whole kernel corn
- 1/2 teaspoon ground cumin
- 1/8 teaspoon ground black pepper
- 1 5-ounce can or one 3-1/2-ounce package whole baby clams, drained
- 1/8 cup snipped fresh cilantro
- 1/2 dash cracked black pepper

Directions:

1. Thaw frozen halibut and scallops.
2. Halibut should be cut into 1-inch pieces, and large scallops should be sliced in half or halves; leave aside.

3. Heat the oil in a big saucepan over medium heat.
4. Cook, turning periodically, for 5 minutes or until onion, sweet pepper, and garlic are soft. In a large mixing bowl, combine the tomatoes, vegetable broth, water, corn, cumin, and ground black pepper. Bring to a boil, and then turn off the heat.
5. Cook for 10 minutes with the lid on.
6. Step 2
7. Toss the halibut and scallops into the tomato sauce. Return to a boil, and then lower the heat.
8. Cook for another 2 to 3 minutes, uncovered, or until the scallops are opaque and the halibut flakes readily when probed with a fork.
9. Step 3
10. Just before serving, add the clams and cilantro.
11. Season with cracked black pepper, if preferred.

Per serving: Calories: 336 Kcal; Fat: 9.3 g; Carbs: 43.5 g; Protein: 24.1 g: Sodium: 522 mg; Sugar: 11 g

123. Salmon with Horseradish Pistachio Crust

Preparation time: 20 minutes
Cooking time: 10 minutes
Servings: 6
Ingredients:
- 6 salmon fillets (4 ounces each)
- 1/3 cup sour cream
- 1 to 2 tablespoons prepared horseradish
- 1 tablespoon snipped fresh dill or 1 teaspoon dill weed
- 1/2 cup minced shallots
- 2 tablespoons olive oil
- 1/4 teaspoon crushed red pepper flakes
- 1 garlic clove, minced
- 1/2 teaspoon grated lemon or orange zest
- 2/3 cup dry bread crumbs
- 2/3 cup chopped pistachios

Directions:
1. Preheat the oven to 350 degrees Fahrenheit.
2. Place the salmon, skin side down, in a 15x10x1-inch baking pan that has not been buttered. Sour cream should be spread over each fillet.
3. Combine the remaining ingredients in a bowl.
4. Press the crumb-nut mixture onto the tops of the salmon fillets to help the coating adhere.
5. 12-15 minutes in the oven, until the fish begins to flake easily with a fork.

Per serving: Calories: 376 Kcal; Fat: 25 g; Carbs: 15 g; Protein: 24 g: Sodium: 219 mg; Sugar: 3 g

124. Crab Cake Egg Stacks

Preparation time: 40 minutes
Cooking time: 30 minutes
Servings: 5
Ingredients:
- 1 teaspoon lemon juice
- 5 eggs, poached
- Bottled hot pepper sauce
- 1/4 cup snipped fresh cilantro (Optional)
- 1 6-ounce pouch refrigerated lump crabmeat, rinse, drain and flake
- 1 cup shredded zucchini
- Nonstick cooking spray
- 1 avocado, halved, seeded, peeled and chopped
- 2 tablespoons mango chutney
- 1/4 teaspoon ground black pepper
- 1/4 teaspoon crushed red pepper
- 2 egg whites
- 2 tablespoons plain fat-free Greek yogurt
- 3 tablespoons whole-wheat panko

- ½ teaspoon chili powder

Directions:

1. Combine crabmeat, zucchini, egg whites, and yoghurt in a medium mixing dish.
2. Combine the panko, chili powder, black pepper, and crushed red pepper in a mixing bowl.
3. Form the mixture into five 1/2-inch-thick patties (each patty should have about 1/3 cup crab mixture). Using cooking spray, coat a large nonstick skillet.
4. Preheat the skillet to medium-high. Cook patties in a heated skillet for 10 minutes, or until gently browned (160 degrees F), rotating once halfway through.
5. Reduce the heat as needed to keep the patties from browning too much.
6. Meanwhile, combine avocado, chutney, and lemon juice in a small bowl for the avocado topper.
7. Each crab cake should be topped with a poached egg.
8. Toss the avocado topper on top of everything.
9. Add 1 or 2 dashes of hot pepper sauce to each serving.
10. Garnish with trimmed fresh cilantro if desired.

Per serving: Calories: 193 Kcal; Fat: 9 g; Carbs: 12 g; Protein: 16 g: Sodium: 310 mg; Sugar: 5 g

125. Crunchy Baked Fish

Preparation time: 10 minutes
Cooking time: 20 minutes
Servings: 4
Ingredients:

- ½ cup cornflake crumbs
- 2 tablespoons juice of half a lemon
- 3 tablespoons lemon pepper blend
- 4 (4 ounce) tilapia or catfish fillets
- 1 Cooking spray

Directions:

1. Preheat the oven to 350 degrees Fahrenheit. Spray a 9 x 9 x 2 inch baking pan with cooking spray.
2. Fill the pan with fillets. 1 tbsp. evenly sprinkled over the tops of the fish Lemon Pepper Blend Mrs. Dash® Lemon juice should be squeezed over the fish.
3. Toss the remaining 2 tablespoons of Mrs. Dash® Lemon Pepper Blend with the corn flake crumbs. Sprinkle the corn flake crumbs on top of the fillets with care.
4. Preheat the oven to 200°F and bake the fish for 20 minutes, or until fork tender.

Per serving: Calories: 156 Kcal; Fat: 1.5 g; Carbs: 10.9 g; Protein: 23.7 g: Sodium: 135.7 mg; Sugar: 0.4 g

126. Prawns Puttanesca

Preparation time: 15 minutes
Cooking time: 15 minutes
Servings: 8
Ingredients:

- 2 tablespoons olive oil
- 2 1/2 pounds prawns (about 16 large shrimp), peeled and deveined
- 1 teaspoon freshly ground black pepper
- 4 tablespoons dry white wine
- 8 tomatoes, peeled and seeded, then diced (about 2 1/2 cups)
- 1/2 cup dry-packed sun-dried tomatoes, soak in water to rehydrate, drain and chop
- 6 cloves garlic, minced
- 1/2 cup chopped pitted Nicoise olives
- 2 tablespoons capers, rinsed and chopped
- 4 anchovy fillets, rinsed and finely chopped
- 2 tablespoons grated lemon zest
- 2 tablespoons chopped fresh flat-leaf (Italian) parsley

- 2 tablespoons chopped fresh basil
- 1 teaspoon red pepper flakes (optional)

Directions:

1. Heat the olive oil in a large nonstick saute or frying pan over medium-high heat.
2. Cook for 3 minutes after adding the prawns and seasoning with black pepper.
3. Cook for another 2 minutes, or until the prawns are opaque and pink.
4. Place in a bowl and set aside to keep warm.
5. Deglaze the pan with the wine, scraping away any browned bits with a wooden spoon.
6. Toss in the sun-dried and fresh tomatoes, as well as the garlic.
7. Reduce the heat to medium-low and cook for 3 minutes, or until the tomatoes are soft.
8. To enable the flavors to mix, add the remaining ingredients and simmer for another 2 minutes.
9. Return the prawns to the pan and toss them around to evenly coat them.
10. Serve right away.

Per serving: Calories: 218 Kcal; Fat: 6 g; Carbs: 10 g; Protein: 31 g: Sodium: 379 mg; Sugar: 0 g

127. Quick Bean and Tuna Salad

Preparation time: 15 minutes

Cooking time: 10 minutes

Servings: 8

Ingredients:

- 1 whole-grain baguette, torn into 2-inch pieces
- 4 tablespoons olive oil
- 2 cans cannellini beans, no salt added, drained and rinsed
- 1/2 teaspoon pepper
- 2 cans water-packed tuna, no salt added, drain and rinsed

- 4 tablespoons finely chopped fresh parsley
- 4 small dill pickles, cut into bite-size pieces
- 2 small red onions, thinly sliced
- 4 tablespoons red wine vinegar

Directions:

1. Preheat the broiler. Brush 1 tablespoon of the oil over the baguette slices on a sturdy cookie sheet.
2. Place under the broiler for 1–2 minutes, or until golden brown.
3. Broil for a further 1 or 2 minutes after turning the bread pieces.
4. Combine the remaining oil, beans, pickles, onion, vinegar, and pepper in a large mixing basin. Fold in the pieces of broiled baguette.
5. Top with tuna and parsley and divide the mixture among four bowls.

Per serving: Calories: 316 Kcal; Fat: 10 g; Carbs: 23 g; Protein: 19 g: Sodium: 171 mg; Sugar 6 g

128. Quinoa Risotto with Arugula and Parmesan

Preparation time: 20 minutes

Cooking time: 30 minutes

Servings: 6

Ingredients:

- 1 small carrot, peeled and finely shredded
- 1/4 cup grated Parmesan cheese
- 1/4 teaspoon salt
- 1 garlic clove, minced
- 1 cup quinoa, well rinsed
- 1/4 teaspoon freshly ground black pepper
- 1 tablespoon olive oil
- 1/2 yellow onion, chopped
- 1/2 cup thinly sliced fresh shiitake mushrooms

- 2 1/4 cups low-sodium vegetable stock or broth
- 2 cups chopped, stemmed arugula

Directions:

1. Heat the olive oil in a big saucepan over medium heat.
2. Add the onion and cook for 4 minutes, or until tender and transparent.
3. Cook for 1 minute, stirring regularly, after adding the garlic and quinoa. Allowing the garlic to brown is not a good idea.
4. Bring the stock to a boil, and then remove from the heat.
5. Reduce the heat to low and cook for 12 minutes, or until the quinoa is almost cooked but still somewhat firm in the center. It will be a brothy combination.
6. Stir in the arugula, carrots, and mushrooms, and continue to cook for another 2 minutes, or until the quinoa grains have gone transparent.
7. Season with salt, pepper, and stir in the cheese. Serve right away.

Per serving: Calories: 161 Kcal; Fat: 5 g; Carbs: 22 g; Protein: 6 g: Sodium: 211 mg; Sugar: 2 g

129. Roasted Salmon

Preparation time: 15 minutes
Cooking time: 15 minutes
Servings: 2
Ingredients:

- 2 teaspoons extra-virgin olive oil
- 2, 5-ounce pieces salmon with skin
- 1 tablespoon fresh tarragon leaves (optional)
- 1 tablespoon chopped chives

Directions:

1. Preheat the oven to 425 degrees Fahrenheit. Line a baking pan with foil.
2. Take 2 teaspoons oil, rubbed all over the salmon.

3. Roast until the fish is cooked through, about 12 minutes, skin side down on a foil-lined baking sheet.
4. Check if the salmon flakes readily with a fork after 10 minutes.
5. Continue baking for another 2 minutes if it does not flake
6. Lift the salmon off the skin with a metal spatula and set it on a serving platter.
7. Skin should be discarded.
8. Serve the salmon with herb garnish.

Per serving: Calories: 244 Kcal; Fat: 14 g; Carbs: 0.1 g; Protein: 28 g: Sodium: 63 mg; Sugar: 0.6

130. Roasted Salmon with Maple Glaze

Preparation time: 10 minutes
Cooking time: 20 minutes
Servings: 6
Ingredients:

- 2 pounds salmon, cut into 6 equal-sized fillets
- 1/4 teaspoon kosher or sea salt
- 1/4 cup maple syrup
- 1 garlic clove, minced
- 1/4 cup balsamic vinegar
- 1/8 teaspoon fresh cracked black pepper
- Fresh mint or parsley for garnish

Directions:

1. Preheat the oven to 450 degrees Fahrenheit. Using cooking spray, lightly coat a baking pan.
2. Combine the maple syrup, garlic, and balsamic vinegar in a small saucepan over low heat.
3. Remove from heat after only a few minutes of heating.
4. Half of the mixture should go into a small bowl for basting, and the rest should be saved for later.
5. Dry the salmon with a paper towel.

6. On the baking sheet, place the skin-side down. Brush the maple syrup mixture over the salmon.
7. Bake for 10 minutes, then baste with the maple syrup mixture and bake for 5 minutes more.
8. Continue to baste and bake for another 20 to 25 minutes or until the salmon flakes easily.
9. Place the salmon fillets on serving dishes. Season with salt and black pepper, then drizzle with the maple syrup mixture you set aside.
10. Serve immediately with fresh mint or parsley as a garnish.

Per serving: Calories: 257 Kcal; Fat: 10 g; Carbs: 10 g; Protein: 30 g: Sodium: 167 mg; Sugar: 8 g

131. Seasoned Baked Cod

Preparation time: 10 minutes
Cooking time: 10 minutes
Servings: 2
Ingredients:
- 2 cod fillets, each 4 to 5 ounces
- 1/2 lemon, cut into 2 wedges
- 1/2 teaspoon old bay seasoning or any other seasoning blend

Directions:
1. Preheat the oven to 350 degrees Fahrenheit. Using cooking spray, lightly coat 4 pieces of aluminum foil.
2. Each piece of aluminum foil should have a cod fillet on it.
3. Sprinkle each fillet with Old Bay Seasoning after squeezing a lemon wedge over it.
4. Wrap the aluminum foil around the fish and secure it in place.
5. Bake for about 10 minutes, or until the fish is opaque t when checked with the tip of a knife.
6. Serve right away.

Per serving: Calories: 90 Kcal; Fat: 1 g; Carbs: 0.1 g; Protein: 20 g: Sodium: 220 mg; Sugar 0.1 g

132. Baked Lemon Salmon

Preparation time: 5 minutes
Cooking time: 20 minutes
Servings: 4
Ingredients:
- 1 pound salmon fillet
- Nonstick cooking spray
- ¼ teaspoon dried thyme
- ½ teaspoon freshly ground black pepper
- Zest and juice of ½ lemon
- ¼ teaspoon salt

Directions:
1. Preheat the oven to 425 degrees Fahrenheit (220 degrees Celsius). Using nonstick cooking spray, coat a baking sheet.
2. In a small bowl, combine the thyme, lemon zest and juice, salt, and pepper and whisk to combine.
3. Arrange the salmon on the prepared baking sheet, skin side down. Pour the thyme mixture over the salmon and evenly distribute it.
4. Bake for 15 to 20 minutes in a preheated oven, or until the fish readily flakes apart.
5. Warm the dish before serving.

Per serving: Calories: 162 Kcal; Fat: 7.0 g; Carbs: 1.0 g; Protein: 2.3 g: Sodium: 166 mg; Sugar 0.7 g

133. Baked Salmon with Basil and Tomato

Preparation time: 10 minutes
Cooking time: 20 minutes
Servings: 2
Ingredients:
- 1 tablespoon olive oil

- 2 tablespoons grated Parmesan
- 2 boneless salmon fillets
- 1 tablespoon dried basil
- 1 tomato, thinly sliced
- cheese
- Nonstick cooking spray

Directions:

1. Preheat the oven to 375 degrees Fahrenheit (190 degrees Celsius).
2. Spray a baking pan with nonstick cooking spray and line it with aluminum foil.
3. Arrange the salmon fillets on the foil and top with basil leaves.
4. Drizzle the olive oil on top of the tomato slices.
5. Serve with grated Parmesan cheese on top.
6. Cook for 20 minutes, or until the meat is opaque and readily flakes apart.

Per serving: Calories: 403 Kcal; Fat: 26.5 g; Carbs: 3.8 g; Protein: 3.6 g: Sodium: 179 mg; Sugar: 0 g

134. Honey-Mustard Roasted Salmon

Preparation time: 5 minutes

Cooking time: 15 minutes

Servings: 4

Ingredients:

- 1 tablespoon honey
- ¼ teaspoon salt
- 2 tablespoons whole-grain mustard
- 2 garlic cloves, minced
- ¼ teaspoon freshly ground black pepper
- 1 pound salmon fillet
- Nonstick cooking spray

Directions:

1. Preheat the oven to 425 degrees Fahrenheit (220 degrees Celsius). Using nonstick cooking spray, coat a baking sheet.
2. In a small bowl, combine the mustard, garlic, honey, salt, and pepper.
3. Place the salmon fillet on the prepared baking sheet, skin-side down.
4. Apply the mustard mixture on the salmon fillet evenly.
5. Roast for 15 to 20 minutes, or until it flakes easily and achieves an internal temperature of 145°F (63°C) in a preheated oven.

Per serving: Calories: 185 Kcal; Fat: 7 g; Carbs: 5.8 g; Protein: 23.2 g: Sodium: 311 mg; Sugar: 4.3 g

135. Salmon and Mushroom Hash with Pesto

Preparation time: 15 minutes

Cooking time: 20 minutes

Servings: 6

Ingredients:

Pesto:

- ½ cup water
- ¼ teaspoon salt, plus additional as needed
- ¼ cup extra-virgin olive oil
- 1 bunch fresh basil
- Juice and zest of 1 lemon

Hash:

- 1 pound wild salmon, cubed
- 2 tablespoons extra-virgin olive oil
- 6 cups mixed mushrooms, sliced

Directions:

1. In a blender or food processor, combine the olive oil, basil, juice and zest, water, and salt until smooth. Remove from the equation.
2. In a large skillet, heat the olive oil over medium heat.
3. Cook for 6 to 8 minutes, or until the mushrooms start to release their juices.
4. Cook for 5 to 6 minutes on each side until the salmon is cooked through.

5. Stir in the pesto that has been produced. Taste and season with more salt if necessary. Serve immediately.

Per serving: Calories: 264 Kcal; Fat: 14.7 g; Carbs: 30.9 g; Protein: 7.0 g: Sodium: 480 mg; Sugar: 5 g

136. Spiced Citrus Sole

Preparation time: 10 minutes
Cooking time: 10 minutes
Servings: 4
Ingredients:

- 1 teaspoon garlic powder
- 1 teaspoon chili powder
- Pinch sea salt
- 2 teaspoons freshly squeezed lime juice
- 4 sole fillets, patted dry
- 1 tablespoon extra-virgin olive oil
- ½ teaspoon lemon zest
- ½ teaspoon lime zest
- ¼ teaspoon smoked paprika
- ¼ teaspoon freshly ground black pepper

Directions:

1. Preheat the oven to 450 degrees Fahrenheit (235 degrees Celsius).
2. Set aside an aluminum foil-lined baking sheet.
3. In a small mixing bowl, add the garlic powder, chili powder, lemon zest, lime zest, paprika, pepper, and salt.
4. Place the sole fillets on the prepared baking sheet and rub the spice mixture all over them until they are evenly coated.
5. Drizzle the fillets with the olive oil and lime juice.
6. Preheat the oven to 350°F and bake for about 8 minutes, or until flaky.
7. Remove from the heat and transfer to a serving platter.

Per serving: Calories: 183 Kcal; Fat: 5 g; Carbs: 0 g; Protein: 32.1 g: Sodium: 136 mg; Sugar: 0 g

137. Crispy Tilapia with Mango Salsa

Preparation time: 5 minutes
Cooking time: 10 minutes
Servings: 2
Ingredients:

Salsa:

- 1 cup chopped mango
- 2 tablespoons chopped fresh cilantro
- 2 tablespoons chopped red onion
- 2 tablespoons freshly squeezed lime juice
- ½ jalapeño pepper, seeded and minced
- Pinch salt

Tilapia:

- ½ teaspoon garlic powder
- ¼ teaspoon salt
- 1 tablespoon paprika
- 1 teaspoon onion powder
- 2 teaspoons extra-virgin olive oil
- ½ teaspoon dried thyme
- ½ teaspoon freshly ground black pepper
- ¼ teaspoon cayenne pepper
- ½ pound boneless tilapia fillets
- 1 lime, cut into wedges, for serving

Directions:

1. Toss the mango, cilantro, onion, lime juice, jalapeno, and salt together in a medium bowl. Remove from the equation.
2. Prepare the tilapia as follows: In a small mixing bowl, combine the paprika, onion powder, thyme, black pepper, cayenne pepper, garlic powder, and salt.
3. Brush both sides of the fillets with the mixture.
4. In a large skillet, heat the olive oil over medium heat.

Per serving: Calories: 239 Kcal; Fat: 7.8 g; Carbs: 21.9 g; Protein: 25 g: Sodium: 416 mg; Sugar: 3 g

138. Mediterranean Grilled Sea Bass

Preparation time: 20 minutes
Cooking time: 20 minutes
Servings: 6
Ingredients:

- 2 pounds sea bass
- 3 tablespoons extra-virgin olive oil, divided
- 2 large cloves garlic, chopped
- ¼ teaspoon onion powder
- ¼ teaspoon garlic powder
- Lemon pepper and sea salt to taste
- 1 tablespoon chopped Italian flat leaf parsley
- ¼ teaspoon paprika

Directions:

1. Heat the grill to a high setting.
2. In a large mixing bowl, add the onion powder, garlic powder, paprika, lemon pepper, and sea salt.
3. Dredge the fish in the spice mixture and turn to coat well.
4. In a small skillet, heat 2 tablespoons olive oil.
5. Cook for 1 to 2 minutes, stirring regularly, after adding the garlic and parsley.
6. Turn off the heat and set the skillet aside.
7. Brush the remaining 1 tablespoon olive oil on the grill grates lightly.
8. Cook the fish for around 7 minutes on the grill.
9. Cook for an additional 7 minutes after flipping the fish and drizzled with the garlic mixture or until the fish flakes easily when lightly tapped with a fork.

Per serving: Calories: 200 Kcal; Fat: 10.3 g; Carbs: 0.6 g; Protein: 26 g: Sodium: 105 mg; Sugar: 0 g

139. Baked Halibut Steaks with Vegetables

Preparation time: 15 minutes
Cooking time: 20 minutes
Servings: 4
Ingredients:

- ¼ teaspoon ground black pepper
- 4 halibut steaks
- 2 teaspoon olive oil, divided
- 1 clove garlic, peeled and minced
- 2 cups diced fresh tomatoes
- 2 tablespoons chopped fresh basil
- ¼ teaspoon salt
- $^1/_3$ cup crumbled feta cheese
- ½ cup minced onion
- 1 cup diced zucchini

Directions:

1. Preheat the oven to 450 degrees Fahrenheit (235 degrees Celsius). 1 teaspoon olive oil, lightly coated in a shallow baking dish
2. Heat the remaining 1 teaspoon of olive oil in a medium saucepan.
3. Mix in the garlic, onion, and zucchini thoroughly.
4. Cook, stirring periodically, for 5 minutes, or until the zucchini is softened.
5. Stir in the tomatoes, basil, salt, and pepper after removing the saucepan from the heat.
6. Arrange the halibut steaks in a single layer in the greased baking dish. Using a spatula, evenly distribute the zucchini mixture over the steaks. Feta cheese should be strewn across the top.
7. Bake for 15 minutes in a preheated oven, or until the fish flakes easily when

lightly poked with a fork. Serve immediately.

Per serving: Calories: 258 Kcal; Fat: 7.6 g; Carbs: 6.5 g; Protein: 38.6 g: Sodium: 384 mg; Sugar: 4 g

140. Spicy Haddock Stew

Preparation time: 15 minutes

Cooking time: 35 minutes

Servings: 6

Ingredients:

- 1 cup low-sodium chicken broth
- ¼ teaspoon red pepper flakes
- ¼ cup coconut oil
- 1 tablespoon minced garlic
- ½ fennel bulb, thinly sliced
- 1 carrot, diced
- 1 sweet potato, diced
- 2 tablespoons chopped fresh cilantro, for garnish
- 1 can low-sodium diced tomatoes
- 1 onion, chopped
- 2 celery stalks, chopped
- 1 cup coconut milk
- 12 ounces haddock, cut into 1-inch chunks

Directions:

1. Heat the coconut oil in a large saucepan over medium-high heat.
2. Sauté for about 4 minutes, stirring periodically, or until the garlic, onion, and celery are soft.
3. Sauté for another 4 minutes after adding the fennel bulb, carrot, and sweet potato.
4. Stir in the diced tomatoes, coconut milk, chicken broth, and red pepper flakes before bringing the mixture to a boil.
5. Reduce the heat to low and cook for about 15 minutes, or until the vegetables are fork-tender, once it begins to boil.
6. Add the haddock chunks and heat for another 10 minutes, or until the fish is fully cooked.
7. Before serving, sprinkle the cilantro on top as a garnish.

Per serving: Calories: 276 Kcal; Fat: 20.9 g; Carbs: 6.8 g; Protein: 14.2 g: Sodium: 226 mg; Sugar: 2 g

Chapter 8: Meat Recipes: Meat, Pork, Lamb, Poultry

141. Asian Pork Tenderloin

Preparation time: 20 minutes
Cooking time: 20 minutes
Servings: 4
Ingredients:

- 2 tablespoons sesame seeds
- 1 teaspoon ground coriander
- 1/2 teaspoon minced onion
- 1 tablespoon sesame oil
- 1 pound pork tenderloin, sliced into 4 portions
- 1/8 teaspoon ground cinnamon
- 1/8 teaspoon cayenne pepper
- 1/8 teaspoon celery seed
- 1/4 teaspoon ground cumin

Directions:

1. Preheat the oven to 400 degrees Fahrenheit. Using cooking spray, lightly coat a baking dish.
2. Place the sesame seeds in a single layer in a heavy frying pan.
3. Cook the seeds, stirring regularly, over low heat until they become golden and provide a toasted scent, about 1 to 2 minutes.
4. Remove the seeds from the pan and set them aside to cool.
5. Combine Coriander, cayenne pepper, celery seed, minced onion, cumin, cinnamon, sesame oil, and toasted sesame seeds in a bowl.
6. Stir to ensure that everything is uniformly distributed.
7. Place the pork tenderloin in the baking dish that has been prepared. Spices should be applied to both sides of the pork chunks.
8. Bake for 15 minutes, or until no longer pink. Alternatively, bake until a meat thermometer reads 165 F (medium) or 170 F (well done).

Per serving: Calories: 176 Kcal; Fat: 8 g; Carbs: 1 g; Protein: 25 g: Sodium: 61 mg; Sugar: 0 g

142. Baked chicken and Wild Rice

Preparation time: 20 minutes
Cooking time: 70 minutes
Servings: 6
Ingredients:

- 1 pound boneless, skinless chicken breast halves
- 2 cups unsalted chicken broth
- 1 1/2 cups chopped celery
- 1 1/2 cups whole pearl onions
- 3/4 cup uncooked long-grain white rice
- 1 teaspoon fresh tarragon
- 3/4 cup uncooked wild rice
- 1 1/2 cups dry white wine

Directions:

1. Preheat the oven to 300 degrees Fahrenheit.
2. Chicken breasts should be cut into 1-inch chunks.
3. Combine the chicken, celery, onions, and tarragon in a nonstick frying pan with 1 cup unsalted chicken stock.
4. Cook for about 10 minutes over medium heat or until the chicken and vegetables are cooked. Allow to cool before serving.
5. Combine the rice, wine, and the remaining 1 cup chicken broth in a baking dish. Allow 30 minutes to soak.
6. In a baking dish, combine the chicken and vegetables.
7. Bake for 60 minutes with the lid on. If the rice becomes too dry, keep an eye on it and add more liquid as needed.

8. Serve right away.

Per serving: Calories: 313 Kcal; Fat: 3 g; Carbs: 38 g; Protein: 23 g: Sodium: 104 mg; Sugar: 2 g

143. Grilled Lemon Chicken

Preparation time: 10 minutes

Cooking time: 12 minutes

Servings: 2

Ingredients:

- ½ teaspoon dried thyme
- ¼ teaspoon salt
- 2 boneless, skinless chicken breasts
- 4 tablespoons freshly squeezed lemon juice
- 1 teaspoon dried basil
- 1 teaspoon paprika
- ¼ teaspoon garlic powder
- 2 tablespoons olive oil, plus more for greasing the grill grates

Directions:

1. In a large mixing bowl, whisk together the lemon juice, olive oil, basil, paprika, thyme, salt, and garlic powder until well mixed.
2. Allow the chicken breasts to marinade in the bowl for at least 30 minutes.
3. Preheat the grill to medium-high heat when ready to cook.
4. Grease the grill grates lightly with olive oil.
5. Remove the chicken breasts from the marinade and place them on the grill grates.
6. Cook for 12 to 14 minutes, flipping halfway through, or until a meat thermometer placed in the center of the chicken registers 165 degrees Fahrenheit (74 degrees Celsius).
7. Allow 5 minutes for the chicken to cool before serving heated.

Per serving: Calories: 251 Kcal; Fat: 15.5 g; Carbs: 1.9 g; Protein: 27.3 g: Sodium: 371 mg; Sugar: 0.2 g

144. Quick Chicken Salad Wraps

Preparation time: 15 minutes

Cooking time: 0 minutes

Servings: 2

Ingredients:

Tzatziki Sauce:

- 1 teaspoon dried dill
- Salt and freshly ground black pepper, to taste
- 1 tablespoon freshly squeezed lemon juice
- Pinch garlic powder
- ½ cup plain Greek yogurt

Salad Wraps:

- ½ English cucumber, peeled if desired and thinly sliced
- ¼ cup pitted black olives
- 2 (8-inch) whole-grain pita bread
- 1 cup shredded chicken meat
- 2 roasted red bell peppers, thinly sliced
- 1 scallion, chopped
- 2 cups mixed greens

Directions:

1. To make the tzatziki sauce, combine the yoghurt, lemon juice, garlic powder, dill, salt, and pepper in a mixing bowl and whisk until creamy and smooth.
2. Place the pita bread on a clean work area and ladle 14 cup of tzatziki sauce over each piece, spreading it evenly.
3. Shredded chicken, mixed greens, red pepper slices, cucumber slices, black olives, and chopped scallion are served on top.
4. Enjoy the salad wraps rolled up.

Per serving: Calories: 428 Kcal; Fat: 10.6 g; Carbs: 50.9 g; Protein: 31.1 g: Sodium: 675 mg; Sugar: 3 g

145. Roasted Chicken Thighs With Basmati Rice

Preparation time: 15 minutes
Cooking time: 50 minutes
Servings: 2
Ingredients:
Chicken:

- ½ teaspoon cumin
- ½ teaspoon cinnamon
- ¼ teaspoon garlic powder
- ¼ teaspoon coriander
- ½ teaspoon paprika
- ⅛ teaspoon cayenne pepper
- 10 ounces boneless, skinless chicken thighs (about 4 pieces)
- ¼ teaspoon ginger powder
- ¼ teaspoon salt

Rice:

- 2 pinches saffron
- 1 cup low-sodium chicken stock
- 1 tablespoon olive oil
- ¼ teaspoon salt
- ½ small onion, minced
- ½ cup basmati rice

Directions:

1. Preheat the oven to 350 degrees Fahrenheit (180 degrees Celsius).
2. In a small mixing bowl, combine the cumin, cinnamon, paprika, ginger powder, garlic powder, coriander, salt, and cayenne pepper.
3. Rub the spice mixture all over the chicken thighs with your hands.
4. In a baking dish, place the chicken thighs. Roast for 35 to 40 minutes in a preheated oven, or until an internal temperature of 165°F (74°C) is reached on a meat thermometer.
5. Meanwhile, in a skillet over medium-high heat, heat the olive oil.
6. Cook, stirring periodically, for 5 minutes, or until the onion is aromatic.

7. Combine the basmati rice, saffron, chicken stock, and salt in a pot. Reduce to a low heat, cover, and cook for 15 minutes, or until light and fluffy.
8. Take the chicken out of the oven and place it on a platter with the rice.

Per serving: Calories: 400 Kcal; Fat: 9.6 g; Carbs: 40.2 g; Protein: 37.2 g: Sodium: 714 mg; Sugar: 0 g

146. Herbed-Mustard-Coated Pork Tenderloin

Preparation time: 10 minutes
Cooking time: 15 minutes
Servings: 4
Ingredients:

- 6 garlic cloves
- ½ teaspoon sea salt
- 3 tablespoons fresh rosemary leaves
- ¼ cup Dijon mustard
- ½ cup fresh parsley leaves
- 1 tablespoon extra-virgin olive oil
- 1 pork tenderloin
- ¼ teaspoon freshly ground black pepper

Directions:

1. Preheat the oven to 400 degrees Fahrenheit (205 degrees Celsius).
2. In a food processor, combine all of the ingredients except the pork tenderloin. Pulse until a thick consistency is achieved.
3. Place the pork tenderloin on a baking sheet and coat well with the mixture.
4. Place the sheet in the preheated oven and bake for 15 minutes, or until the pork reaches an internal temperature of 165°F (74°C). Flip the tenderloin halfway through the cooking period. .
5. Place the cooked pork tenderloin on a large plate and set aside for 5 minutes to cool before serving.

Per serving: Calories: 363 Kcal; Fat: 18.1 g; Carbs: 4.9 g; Protein: 2.2 g: Sodium: 514 mg; Sugar; 0.0

147. Grilled Chicken and Zucchini Kebabs

Preparation time: 10 minutes
Cooking time: 20 minutes
Servings: 4
Ingredients:

- 1 pound boneless and skinless chicken breasts, cut into 1½-inch pieces
- 2 medium zucchini, cut into 1-inch pieces
- ¼ cup extra-virgin olive oil
- 2 tablespoons balsamic vinegar
- ½ cup Kalamata olives, pitted and halved
- ¼ cup torn fresh basil leaves
- Nonstick cooking spray
- 2 tablespoons olive brine
- 1 teaspoon dried oregano, crushed between your fingers

Special Equipment:

- 14 to 15 (12-inch) wooden skewers, soaked for at least 30 minutes

Directions:

1. Spray nonstick cooking spray on the grill grates. Preheat your grill to medium-high.
2. Whisk together the olive oil, vinegar, and oregano in a small basin. Divide the marinade into two large zip-top plastic bags.
3. Put the zucchini in one bag and the chicken in the other. Both the chicken and the zucchini should be sealed and massaged with the marinade.
4. Thread 6 wooden skewers with the chicken. Using 8 or 9 wooden skewers, thread the zucchini.
5. Grill the kebabs in batches for 5 minutes on one side, then flip and cook for another 5 minutes, or until the chicken juices run clear.
6. Transfer the skewered chicken and zucchini to a wide serving bowl. Combine the olives, olive brine, and basil in a mixing bowl.

Per serving: Calories: 283 Kcal; Fat: 15.0 g; Carbs: 26.0 g; Protein: 11 g: Sodium: 575 mg; Sugar: 4 g

148. Macadamia Pork

Preparation time: 10 minutes
Cooking time: 10 minutes
Servings: 4
Ingredients:

- 1 cup unsweetened coconut milk
- 1 pork tenderloin, cut into ½-inch slices and pounded thin
- ¼ teaspoon freshly ground black pepper, divided
- ½ cup macadamia nuts
- 1 teaspoon sea salt, divided
- 1 tablespoon extra-virgin olive oil

Directions:

1. Preheat the oven to 400 degrees Fahrenheit (205 degrees Celsius).
2. Season the pork with ½ teaspoon of salt and ½ teaspoon ground black pepper on a clean work surface. Remove from the equation.
3. In a mixing bowl, grind the macadamia nuts with the remaining salt and black pepper in a food processor. Set aside after thoroughly mixing.
4. In a separate bowl, combine the coconut milk and olive oil. Stir everything together thoroughly.
5. Dredge the pork chops in the coconut milk mixture. Plunge them in the macadamia nut mixture to coat them thoroughly. Remove any excess by shaking it off.
6. Place the well-coated pork chops on a baking sheet and bake for 10 minutes,

or until the pork reaches an internal temperature of 165°F (74°C).

7. Immediately transfer the pork chops to a serving platter and serve.

Per serving: Calories: 436 Kcal; Fat: 32.8 g; Carbs: 5.9 g; Protein: 33.1 g: Sodium: 310 mg; Sugar: 4.5 g

149. Almond-Crusted Chicken Tenders with Honey

Preparation time: 10 minutes

Cooking time: 20 minutes

Servings: 4

Ingredients:

- 1 tablespoon honey
- 1 tablespoon whole-grain or Dijon mustard
- 1 cup almonds, roughly chopped
- ¼ teaspoon freshly ground black pepper
- ¼ teaspoon kosher or sea salt
- Nonstick cooking spray
- 1 pound boneless and skinless chicken breast tenders/tenderloins

Directions:

1. Preheat the oven to 425 degrees Fahrenheit (220 degrees Celsius). Using parchment paper, line a large, rimmed baking sheet.
2. Spray a wire cooling rack with nonstick cooking spray and place it on the parchment-lined baking sheet.
3. Combine the honey, mustard, pepper, and salt in a large mixing dish.
4. Toss in the chicken and gently toss to coat. Remove from the equation.
5. Spread the almonds out on a wide sheet of parchment paper.
6. The coated chicken tenders should be pressed into the nuts until they are equally coated on all sides.
7. Place the chicken on the wire rack that has been prepared.

8. Bake for 15 to 20 minutes, or until the internal temperature of the chicken reaches 165°F (74°C) and any juices flow clear when tested with a meat thermometer.
9. Allow for 5 minutes of cooling before serving.

Per serving: Calories: 222 Kcal; Fat: 7.0 g; Carbs: 29 g; Protein: 11 g: Sodium: 448 mg; Sugar: 1 g

150. Parsley-Dijon Chicken and Potatoes

Preparation time: 5 minutes

Cooking time: 22 minutes

Servings: 6

Ingredients:

- 1 cup low-sodium or no-salt-added chicken broth
- 1 cup chopped fresh flat-leaf (Italian) parsley, including stems
- 1 tablespoon extra-virgin olive oil
- 1½ pounds boneless and skinless chicken thighs, pat dry, cut into 1-inch cube
- 1½ pounds potatoes, unpeeled, cut into ½-inch cubes
- 1 tablespoon Dijon mustard
- ¼ teaspoon freshly ground black pepper
- ¼ teaspoon kosher or sea salt
- 2 garlic cloves, minced
- ¼ cup dry white wine
- 1 tablespoon freshly squeezed lemon juice

Directions:

1. Heat the oil in a large skillet over medium-high heat.
2. Cook for 5 minutes with the chicken, stirring just when it has browned on one side.
3. Remove the chicken from the pan and set aside on a platter.

4. Add the potatoes to the skillet and cook for 5 minutes, stirring only after one side has turned golden and crispy.

5. Push the potatoes to the side of the pan, add the garlic, and cook for 1 minute, stirring frequently.

6. Cook for 1 minute, or until the wine has virtually evaporated.

7. Add the chicken stock, mustard, salt, and pepper, as well as the chicken that was set aside. Bring the water to a boil over high heat.

8. When the water boils, cover and cook for 10 to 12 minutes, or until the potatoes are cooked and the internal temperature of the chicken reaches 165°F (74°C) on a meat thermometer and any juices run clear.

9. Stir in the parsley in the last minute of cooking.

10. Remove the pan from the heat and mix in the lemon juice before serving.

Per serving: Calories: 324 Kcal; Fat: 9 g; Carbs: 45 g; Protein: 16 g: Sodium: 560 mg; Sugar: 6 g

151. Gyro Burgers with Tahini Sauce

Preparation time: 15 minutes

Cooking time: 10 minutes

Servings: 4

Ingredients:

- 1 cup thinly sliced red onion
- 4 (6-inch) whole-wheat pita breads, warmed
- 1 pound beef flank steak, (top round steak, or lamb leg steak) about 1 inch thick, center cut
- Nonstick cooking spray
- 2 tablespoons extra-virgin olive oil
- 1 tablespoon dried oregano
- 1 teaspoon ground cumin
- ½ teaspoon freshly ground black pepper
- ¼ teaspoon kosher or sea salt
- 1 medium green bell pepper, halved and seeded
- 2 tablespoons tahini or peanut butter
- 1¼ teaspoons garlic powder, divided
- 1 tablespoon hot water (optional)
- ½ cup plain Greek yogurt
- 1 tablespoon freshly squeezed lemon juice

Directions:

1. Place a rack approximately 4 inches below the broiler element in the oven.

2. Preheat the broiler in the oven to high. Aluminum foil should be used to line a big, rimmed baking pan.

3. Spray a wire cooling rack with nonstick cooking spray and place it on top of the foil. Remove from the equation.

4. Whisk together the olive oil, oregano, 1 teaspoon garlic powder, cumin, pepper, and salt in a small basin. 1 teaspoon of the oil mixture should be reserved for rubbing on all sides of the steak.

5. Place the meat on the rack that has been prepared. Place the bell pepper cut-side down on the rack and brush with the remaining oil mixture.

6. To flatten the pepper, press it with the heel of your hand.

7. Cook for 5 minutes under the broiler. Broil for another 2 to 5 minutes, until the pepper is browned and the internal temperature of the steak reaches 145oF (63oC) on a meat thermometer. Rest the pepper and steak for 5 minutes on a chopping board.

8. Meanwhile, whisk the tahini in a separate bowl until smooth (adding 1 tablespoon of hot water if your tahini is sticky).

9. Whisk in the remaining ¼ teaspoon of garlic powder, as well as the yoghurt and lemon juice.

83

10. Cut the meat into 14-inch-thick pieces crosswise. Bell peppers should be sliced into strips.
11. Fill the warm pita breads with the steak, bell pepper, and onion. Serve with a tahini sauce drizzle.

Per serving: Calories: 348 Kcal; Fat: 15 g; Carbs: 20 g; Protein: 33 g: Sodium: 530 mg; Sugar; 11 g

152. Greek-Style Lamb Burgers

Preparation time: 10 minutes
Cooking time: 10 minutes
Servings: 4
Ingredients:

- 4 tablespoons crumbled feta cheese
- 1 pound ground lamb
- ½ teaspoon salt
- Buns, toppings, and tzatziki, for serving (optional)
- ½ teaspoon freshly ground black pepper

Directions:

1. Preheat the grill to a high temperature.
2. Toss the lamb with the salt and pepper in a large mixing dish with your hands.
3. Cut the meat into four equal parts. To construct a top and bottom, divide each part in half.
4. Make a 3-inch circle out of each part. Make a hole in the center of one of the halves and fill it with 1 tablespoon of feta cheese.
5. Place the second half of the patty on top of the feta cheese and press down to combine the two pieces into a spherical burger.
6. For medium-well, grill each side for 3 minutes. Serve on a bun with your favorite toppings and, if preferred, tzatziki sauce.

Per serving: Calories: 345 Kcal; Fat: 29 g; Carbs: 1 g; Protein: 20 g: Sodium: 462 mg; Sugar: 2 g

153. Crispy Pesto Chicken

Preparation time: 15 minutes
Cooking time: 50 minutes
Servings: 2
Ingredients:

- 1 tablespoon olive oil
- 12 ounces small red potatoes, scrubbed and diced into 1-inch pieces
- 1 boneless, skinless chicken breast
- 3 tablespoons prepared pesto
- ½ teaspoon garlic powder
- ¼ teaspoon salt

Directions:

1. Preheat the oven to 425 degrees Fahrenheit (220 degrees Celsius). Line a baking sheet with parchment paper.
2. In a medium mixing bowl, combine the potatoes, olive oil, garlic powder, and salt. Toss thoroughly to coat.
3. Spread the potatoes out on parchment paper and bake for 10 minutes.
4. Roast for another 10 minutes after flipping the potatoes.
5. In the meantime, combine the chicken with the pesto in the same bowl, covering it evenly.
6. Make sure the potatoes are golden brown on both the top and bottom.
7. Return them to the pan and add the chicken breasts.
8. Reduce the heat to 350 degrees Fahrenheit (180 degrees Celsius) and roast the chicken and potatoes for 30 minutes.
9. Check that the chicken has reached an internal temperature of 165 degrees Fahrenheit (74 degrees Celsius) and that the potatoes are fork-tender.
10. Remove from the oven and set aside to cool for 5 minutes before serving.

Per serving: Calories: 378 Kcal; Fat: 16 g; Carbs: 30.1 g; Protein: 29 g: Sodium: 425 mg; Sugar: 3 g

154. Roasted Pork Tenderloin

Preparation time: 15 minutes

Cooking time: 20 minutes

Servings: 2

Ingredients:

- ½ cup fresh cilantro
- ½ teaspoon salt, divided
- Pinch freshly ground black pepper
- 1 pork tenderloin
- ½ cup fresh parsley
- 3 tablespoons freshly squeezed lemon juice
- 6 small garlic cloves
- 3 tablespoons olive oil, divided
- 2 teaspoons cumin
- 1 teaspoon smoked paprika

Directions:

1. Preheat the oven to 425 degrees Fahrenheit (220 degrees Celsius).
2. Combine the cilantro, parsley, garlic, 2 tablespoons olive oil, lemon juice, cumin, paprika, and 14 tsp salt in a food processor.
3. Pulse the mixture 15 to 20 times, or until it is fairly smooth. Scrape down the edges as needed to ensure that all of the components are fully incorporated.
4. Place the sauce in a small mixing dish and put it aside.
5. Sprinkle the remaining ¼ teaspoon of salt and a liberal pinch of black pepper on all sides of the pork tenderloin.
6. In a sauté pan, heat the remaining 1 tablespoon of olive oil.
7. Sear the pork for 3 minutes on each side, turning frequently, until golden brown.
8. Transfer the pork to a baking tray and roast for 15 minutes, or until the internal temperature reaches 145°F (63°C) in a preheated oven.
9. Allow for 5 minutes of cooling before serving.

Per serving: Calories: 169 Kcal; Fat: 13.1 g; Carbs: 2.9 g; Protein: 11 g: Sodium: 322 mg; Sugar: 0 g

155. Lamb Kofta (Spiced Meatballs)

Preparation time: 15 minutes

Cooking time: 30 minutes

Servings: 2

Ingredients:

- ¼ cup walnuts
- ¼ teaspoon cumin
- ¼ teaspoon allspice
- 1 garlic clove
- ½ small onion
- 1 roasted piquillo pepper
- Pinch cayenne pepper
- 8 ounces lean ground lamb
- 2 tablespoons fresh mint
- 2 tablespoons fresh parsley
- ¼ teaspoon salt

Directions:

1. Preheat the oven to 350 degrees Fahrenheit (180 degrees Celsius).
2. Aluminum foil should be used to line a baking pan.
3. Combine the walnuts, garlic, onion, roasted pepper, mint, parsley, cumin, allspice, salt, and cayenne pepper in a food processor.
4. To blend everything, pulse around 10 times.
5. Combine the spice mixture and ground lamb in a large mixing basin. Mix the spices into the meat with your hands or a spatula.
6. Form the lamb into 112-inch balls with your hands (about the size of golf balls).
7. Bake the meatballs for 30 minutes or until they reach an internal temperature

of 165°F (74°C), on the prepared baking sheet.

8. Serve immediately.

Per serving: Calories: 409 Kcal; Fat: 22 g; Carbs: 7.1 g; Protein: 22 g: Sodium: 428mg; Sugar: 2 g

156. Beef and Vegetable Kebabs

Preparation time: 30 minutes

Cooking time: 70 minutes

Servings: 2

Ingredients:

- 1 green pepper, seeded and cut into 4 pieces
- 4 cherry tomatoes
- 1/2 cup brown rice
- 1 small onion, cut into 4 wedges
- 2 cups water
- 4 ounces top sirloin (optional)
- 1 tablespoon fat-free Italian dressing
- 2 wooden skewers, soaked in water for 30 minutes, or metal skewers

Directions:

1. Combine the rice and water in a saucepan over high heat. Bring the water to a boil.
2. Reduce the heat to low, cover, and cook for 30 to 45 minutes, or until the water is absorbed and the rice is soft.
3. If required, add more water to keep the rice from drying out. To keep warm, transfer to a small bowl.
4. Using a sharp knife, cut the meat into four equal chunks. Place the meat in a small bowl and drizzle with Italian dressing. Each item should be rubbed with the dressing.
5. Cover and marinate in the refrigerator for at least 20 minutes, turning occasionally.
6. In a charcoal grill, build a hot fire, or heat a gas grill or a broiler.
7. Spray the grill rack or broiler pan gently with cooking spray away from the heat source. 4 to 6 inches away from the heat source, place the cooking rack.
8. On each skewer, thread 2 beef cubes, 2 green pepper slices, 2 cherry tomatoes, and 2 onion wedges.
9. Place the kebabs on the broiler pan or grill rack. Cook the kebabs for 5 to 10 minutes on the grill or under the broiler, rotating as needed.
10. Using individual dishes, divide the rice.
11. Serve immediately with 1 kebab on top.

Per serving: Calories: 324 Kcal; Fat: 4 g; Carbs: 54 g; Protein: 18 g: Sodium: 142 mg; Sugar: 11 g

157. Spiced Roast Chicken

Preparation time: 15 minutes

Cooking time: 1 hour

Servings: 8

Ingredients:

- ¼ teaspoon paprika
- ¼ teaspoon salt
- 1 (about 3 pounds) whole chicken
- 1 tablespoon olive oil
- 1/8 teaspoon cayenne pepper
- ¼ teaspoon dried basil
- ¼ teaspoon ground black pepper
- ¼ teaspoon dried oregano

Directions:

1. Preheat the oven to 450 degrees Fahrenheit (230 degrees C).
2. Remove all fat from the chicken by rinsing it well inside and out under cold running water. Using paper towels, pat dry.
3. In a small baking pan, place the chicken. Olive oil should be rubbed in. Season the chicken with salt, pepper, oregano, basil, paprika, and cayenne pepper.
4. Cook the chicken for 20 minutes in a preheated oven. Reduce the oven temperature to 400 degrees F (205 degrees C) and continue roasting for another 40 minutes or until the meat

reaches a minimum internal temperature of 165 degrees F (74 degrees C). Allow 10 to 15 minutes to cool before serving.

Per serving: Calories: 229 Kcal; Fat: 14.5 g; Carbs: 0.2 g; Protein: 23 g: Sodium: 142.7 mg; Sugar: 0 g

158. Coconut Chicken Tenders

Preparation time: 15 minutes

Cooking time: 1 hour

Servings: 8

Ingredients:

- 1 pound Chicken tenderloins or chicken breasts, cut into strips.
- Oil for frying
- 1/2 teaspoon salt.
- 1/4 teaspoon pepper.
- 2 eggs.
- 1/2 cup flour.
- Sea salt flakes for garnish, optional.
- 1/2 teaspoon chili powder
- 2/3 cup panko bread crumbs.
- 2 tablespoons water or milk or milk.
- 2/3 cup shredded sweetened coconut flakes.
- Sweet chili sauce for serving.

Directions:

1. Get four wide, shallow bowls out first. Whisk together the flour, chili powder, salt, and pepper in the first bowl.
2. Whisk the eggs and water together in a separate basin (or milk).
3. Place coconut flakes in a third basin and panko bread crumbs in a fourth bowl.
4. Toss the chicken tenders in the flour, then the egg wash, then the coconut flakes, and finally the breadcrumbs. With each step, make sure to coat each chicken tender completely.
5. Pour 1 inch of oil into a large skillet for frying (see comments for baking method). Bring to a simmer over medium heat to bring to temperature.

6. Toss the chicken tenders into the oil with tongs (do not crowd the pan, fry in batches if you need to). Cook for 2-3 minutes, then flip the chicken tenders and cook for a further 3-4 minutes or until golden brown and cooked through.
7. As needed, repeat with the remaining chicken tenders. Allow to cool on a wire cooling rack over paper towels for a few minutes.
8. If desired, sprinkle with sea salt flakes and serve warm with sweet chili dipping sauce.

Per serving: Calories: 161 Kcal; Fat: 5.68 g; Carbs: 0.2 g; Protein: 14 g: Sodium: 798 mg; Sugar: 4.1 g

159. Beef stroganoff

Preparation time: 15 minutes

Cooking time: 15 minutes

Servings: 4

Ingredients:

- 1/2 can fat-free cream of mushroom soup (undiluted)
- 1/2 cup of water
- 1/2 cup chopped onion
- 1/2 pound boneless beef round steak, cut 3/4-inch thick, all fat removed
- 1 tablespoon all-purpose (plain) flour
- 1/2 teaspoon paprika
- 1/2 cup fat-free sour cream
- 4 cups uncooked yolkless egg noodles

Directions:

1. Sauté the onions in a nonstick frying pan over medium heat until they are transparent, about 5 minutes.
2. Continue to cook for another 5 minutes or until the beef is cooked and browned on both sides. Drain the water thoroughly and leave it aside.
3. Bring a big saucepan of water to a boil, 3/4 full of water.
4. Cook for 10 to 12 minutes, or according to package guidelines, until the noodles

are al dente (tender). Drain all of the water from the pasta.

5. Over medium heat, whisk together the soup, water, and flour in a saucepan. Stir for 5 minutes, or until the sauce thickens.

6. Toss the steak in the frying pan with the soup mixture and paprika. Stir the mixture over medium heat until it is thoroughly warmed.

7. Remove the pan from the heat and stir in the sour cream. Stir until everything is well blended.

8. Divide the spaghetti among the dishes to serve. Serve immediately with the beef mixture on top.

Per serving: Calories: 273 Kcal; Fat: 5 g; Carbs: 37 g; Protein: 20 g: Sodium: 193 mg; Sugar: 2 g

160.   Five-spice pork medallions

Preparation time: 15 minutes

Cooking time: 25 minutes

Servings: 4

Ingredients:

- 3/4 teaspoon five-spice powder
- 1 tablespoon olive oil
- 2 tablespoons low-sodium soy sauce
- 1 tablespoon green (spring) onion, including tender green top, minced
- 3 garlic cloves, minced
- 1/2 cup water, plus 1 to 3 tablespoons as needed
- 1/4 cup dry white wine
- 1/3 cup chopped yellow onion
- 1/2 head green cabbage, thinly sliced (about 4 cups)
- 1 tablespoon olive oil
- 1 pound pork tenderloin, trimmed of visible fat
- 1 tablespoon chopped fresh flat-leaf (Italian) parsley

Directions:

1. In a shallow baking dish, mix together the soy sauce, green onion, garlic, olive oil, and five-spice powder to prepare the marinade.

2. To combine ingredients, whisk them together. Toss in the pork and turn to coat.

3. Cover and marinate for at least 2 hours, ideally overnight, in the refrigerator, turning the pork regularly.

4. Preheat the oven to 400 degrees Fahrenheit.

5. Using paper towels blot the pork dry after removing it from the marinade. Remove the marinade and toss it out.

6. Heat the olive oil in a big, oven-safe frying pan over medium-high heat. Cook, rotating as required, until the pork is lightly browned on all sides, about 5 minutes. Fill the pan halfway with water.

7. Place the heating pan in the oven and roast until the pork is slightly pink on the inside and an instant-read thermometer placed in the center registers 160 degrees Fahrenheit.

8. Place the pork on a chopping board and let aside for 10 minutes, covered with a kitchen towel.

9. Place the pan over medium-high heat in the meantime. Deglaze the pan with the wine, scraping away any browned bits with a wooden spoon.

10. Cook for 1 minute after adding the yellow onion. 1 tablespoon of the remaining water and the cabbage are added.

11. Stir well, decrease the heat to medium, cover, and cook for 4 minutes, or until the cabbage has wilted. If necessary, add 1 to 2 teaspoons more water.

12. Make 8 medallions out of the pork tenderloin.

13. Serve the medallions and wilted cabbage on individual dishes with parsley on top. Serve right away.

Per serving: Calories: 219 Kcal; Fat: 11 g; Carbs: 5 g; Protein: 25 g: Sodium: 392 mg; Sugar: 2 g

Chapter 9: Stews and Soups

161. Beef, Tomato, and Lentils Stew

Preparation time: 10 minutes

Cooking time: 10 minutes

Servings: 4

Ingredients:

- 1 tablespoon extra-virgin olive oil
- 1 can chopped tomatoes with garlic and basil, drained
- 1 can lentils, drained
- 1 pound extra-lean ground beef
- 1 onion, chopped
- ⅛ teaspoon freshly ground black pepper
- ½ teaspoon sea salt

Directions:

1. In a medium-high heat pot, heat the olive oil until it shimmers.
2. Cook for 5 minutes, or until the meat is lightly browned, in the pot with the onion.
3. Combine the remaining ingredients in a mixing bowl. Bring the water to a boil.
4. Reduce to medium heat and simmer for another 4 minutes, or until the lentils are cooked. Throughout the cooking process, keep stirring.
5. Transfer to a large serving bowl and serve right away.

Per serving: Calories: 460 Kcal; Fat: 14.8 g; Carbs: 40 g; Protein: 44.2 g; Sodium: 320 mg; Sugar: 5.3 g

162. Potato Lamb and Olive Stew

Preparation time: 20 minutes

Cooking time: 3 hours 42 minutes

Servings: 10

Ingredients:

- 3 sprigs fresh rosemary
- 1 tablespoon lemon zest
- 4 tablespoons almond flour
- ¾ cup low-sodium chicken stock
- 1¼ pounds small potatoes, halved
- 3 cloves garlic, minced
- 4 large shallots, cut into ½-inch wedges
- Coarse sea salt and black pepper, to taste
- 1 cup pitted green olives, halved
- 2 tablespoons extra-virgin olive oil
- ½ cup dry white wine
- 3½ pounds lamb shanks, trim fat and cut crosswise into 1½-inch pieces
- 2 tablespoons lemon juice

Directions:

1. In a mixing dish, combine 1 tablespoon almond flour and 1 cup chicken stock. Stir everything together thoroughly.
2. In a slow cooker, combine the flour mixture, potatoes, garlic, shallots, rosemary, and lemon zest. Season with salt and black pepper to taste. Stir everything together thoroughly. Remove from the equation.
3. In a large mixing basin, combine the remaining almond flour, salt, and black pepper, then submerge the lamb shanks in the flour, and toss to coat.
4. In a nonstick skillet, heat the olive oil over medium-high heat until it shimmers.
5. Cook for 10 minutes, or until golden brown, after adding the well-coated lamb. Halfway through the cooking time, flip the lamb pieces. In a slow cooker, place the cooked lamb.
6. Pour the wine into the same skillet and heat for 2 minutes, or until it has reduced to half its original volume. Fill the slow cooker halfway with wine.

7. Cover the slow cooker and simmer for 3 hours and 30 minutes on high, or until the lamb is extremely tender.
8. Cook the olive halves in the last 20 minutes of cooking by opening the lid and folding them in.
9. Pour the stew onto a large platter and set aside for 5 minutes before skimming any remaining fat from the surface of the broth.
10. Season with salt, pepper, and drizzle with lemon juice. Warm the dish before serving.

Per serving: Calories: 309 Kcal; Fat: 10.3 g; Carbs: 16.1 g; Protein: 36.9 g: Sodium: 239 mg; Sugar: 3.8 g

163. Slow Cook Lamb Shanks with Cannellini Beans Stew

Preparation time: 20 minutes
Cooking time: 10 hours 15 minutes
Servings: 12
Ingredients:

- 1 can cannellini beans, rinsed and drained
- 2 cloves garlic, thinly sliced
- 4 lamb shanks, fat trimmed
- 1 large yellow onion, chopped
- 2 teaspoons tarragon
- ½ teaspoon sea salt
- ¼ teaspoon ground black pepper
- 1 can diced tomatoes, with the juice
- 2 medium-sized carrots, diced
- 1 large stalk celery, chopped

Directions:

1. In a slow cooker, combine the beans, onion, carrots, celery, and garlic. Stir everything together thoroughly.
2. Season the lamb shanks with tarragon, salt, and freshly ground black pepper.
3. Add the tomatoes with their juice, cover, and simmer on high for an hour.

4. Cook for 9 hours on low heat, or until the lamb is quite soft.
5. Place the lamb on a platter and strain the bean mixture into a colander set over a basin to catch the liquid.
6. Allow the liquid to set for 5 minutes before skimming the fat off the surface. Reintroduce the bean mixture to the liquid.
7. Take the bones out of the lamb hot and throw them away. Return the slow cooker to the lamb meat and bean mixture. Cover and reheat for 15 minutes, or until well heated.
8. Transfer to a large serving plate and serve right away.

Per serving: Calories: 317 Kcal; Fat: 9.7 g; Carbs: 7 g; Protein: 52.1 g: Sodium: 375 mg; Sugar: 10 g

164. Beef Stew with Beans and Zucchini

Preparation time: 20 minutes
Cooking time: 6 hours
Servings: 2
Ingredients:

- 8 ounces baby bella mushrooms, quartered
- ¾ cup dry red wine
- ¼ cup minced brined olives
- 2 garlic cloves, minced
- ½ large onion, diced
- 1 can diced or crushed tomatoes with basil
- 1 teaspoon beef base
- 3 tablespoons flour
- 1 can white cannellini beans, drained and rinsed
- ¼ teaspoon salt
- 2 tablespoons olive oil, divided
- 1 pound cubed beef stew meat
- Pinch freshly ground black pepper
- 1 fresh rosemary sprig

- 1 medium zucchini, cut in half lengthwise and then cut into 1-inch pieces.

Directions:

1. Place the tomatoes in a slow cooker with a low heat setting. Stir in the meat foundation until it is fully incorporated.
2. In a large sauté pan, heat 1 tablespoon of olive oil over medium heat.
3. Add the mushrooms, onion, and cook, stirring periodically, for 10 minutes, or until golden.
4. Cook for another 30 seconds after adding the garlic. Fill the slow cooker halfway with vegetables.
5. Combine the stew meat, flour, salt, and pepper in a plastic food storage bag. To blend, close the bag and shake it vigorously.
6. In the sauté pan, heat the remaining 1 tablespoon of olive oil over high heat.
7. Add the floured meat and sear on all sides to form a crust. Add roughly half of the red wine to the pan and scrape up any browned bits on the bottom to deglaze it. Stir the wine to thicken it slightly before transferring it to the slow cooker, along with any leftover wine.
8. To combine the ingredients, stir the stew. Cook for 6 to 8 hours on Low, stirring in the olives and rosemary.
9. Add the beans and zucchini about 30 minutes before the stew is done to warm them up. Warm the dish before serving.

Per serving: Calories: 389 Kcal; Fat: 8 g; Carbs: 25 g; Protein: 30 g: Sodium: 582 mg; Sugar: 3 g

165. Beef Stew with Fennel and Shallots

Preparation time: 30 minutes
Cooking time: 1 hour
Servings: 12

Ingredients:

- 6 tablespoons all-purpose (plain) flour
- 2 pounds boneless lean beef stew meat, trimmed of visible fat and cut into 1 1/2-inch cubes
- 4 tablespoons olive oil or canola oil
- 1 fennel bulb, trimmed and thinly sliced vertically
- 6 large shallots, chopped (about 3 tablespoons)
- 1 1/2 teaspoons ground black pepper, divided
- 4 fresh thyme sprigs
- 2 bay leaf
- 6 cups no-salt-added vegetable stock or broth
- 1 cup red wine, optional (not included in analysis)
- 8 large carrots, peeled and cut into 1-inch chunks
- 8 large red-skinned or white potatoes, peeled and cut into 1-inch chunks
- 36 small boiling onions, about 10 ounces total weight, halved crosswise
- 6 portobello mushrooms, brushed clean and cut into 1-inch chunks
- 1/2 cup finely chopped fresh flat-leaf (Italian) parsley

Directions:

1. On a plate, spread out the flour. Using the flour, dredge the meat cubes. Heat the oil in a large, heavy saucepan over medium heat.
2. Cook, rotating occasionally, until the beef is browned on all sides, about 5 minutes.
3. With a slotted spoon, remove the meat from the pan and set it aside.
4. Over medium heat, add the fennel and onions to the pan and cook until softened and gently brown, about 7 to 8 minutes. 1/4 teaspoon pepper, thyme sprigs, and bay leaf are all good additions. Sauté for one minute.

5. Return the steak to the pan and, if using, add the vegetable stock and wine.
6. Bring to a boil, then reduce to a low heat, cover, and cook until the meat is cooked, about 40 minutes.
7. Combine the carrots, potatoes, onions, and mushrooms in a large mixing bowl.
8. The liquid will not entirely cover the vegetables, but as the mushrooms soften, more liquid will accumulate.
9. Cook for another 30 minutes, or until the vegetables are tender.
10. Remove the bay leaf and thyme sprigs.
11. Combine the parsley and the remaining 1/2 teaspoon pepper in a mixing bowl.
12. Immediately ladle into warmed individual bowls and serve.

Per serving: Calories: 244 Kcal; Fat: 8 g; Carbs: 22 g; Protein: 21 g: Sodium: 185 mg; Sugar: 8 g

166. Beef and Vegetable Stew

Preparation time: 20 minutes

Cooking time: 1 hour

Servings: 6

Ingredients:
- 4 cloves of garlic, chopped
- 1 tablespoon minced fresh parsley
- 1 cup diced carrot
- 1 cup chopped kale
- 2 cups diced yellow onions
- 3 cups low-sodium vegetable or beef stock
- 1 teaspoon dried sage, crushed
- 1/4 cup uncooked barley
- 1/4 cup red wine vinegar
- 1 pound beef round steak
- 2 teaspoons canola oil
- 1/2 cup diced mushrooms
- 1/2 cup diced white potato with skin
- 1 teaspoon dried rosemary, minced
- Black pepper, to taste
- 1 teaspoon balsamic vinegar
- 1 teaspoon minced fresh thyme

- 1 cup diced celery
- 1 cup diced Roma tomatoes
- 1/2 cup diced sweet potato
- 1 tablespoon dried oregano

Directions:
1. Preheat the grill or the broiler (medium heat).
2. Remove the fat and gristle from the steak. Place the steak on the grill or under the broiler, for 12-14 minutes, rotating once. Do not overcook the food.
3. Remove from the pan and set aside to cool while you prepare the vegetables.
4. Sauté vegetables in oil in a large stock pot over medium-high heat until lightly browned, about 10 minutes.
5. Cook for an additional 5 minutes after adding the barley.
6. Using paper towels, pat the meat dry.
7. Add to saucepan after cutting into half-inch pieces.
8. Add the vinegars, stock, herbs, and spices after that.
9. Bring to a boil, then reduce to a low heat and cook for 1 hour, or until the barley is tender and the stew has thickened significantly.

Per serving: Calories: 216 Kcal; Fat:4 g; Carbs: 24 g; Protein: 21 g: Sodium: 138 mg; Sugar: 7 g

167. Tuscan White Bean Stew

Preparation time: 25 minutes

Cooking time: 1 hour

Servings: 4

Ingredients:

For the croutons:
- 1 slice whole-grain bread, cut into 1/2-inch cubes
- 1 tablespoon extra-virgin olive oil
- 2 cloves garlic, quartered

For the soup:
- 1 cup coarsely chopped yellow onion

- 3 carrots, peeled and coarsely chopped
- 1 tablespoon chopped fresh rosemary, plus 6 sprigs
- 1 1/2 cups vegetable stock or broth
- 6 cloves garlic, chopped
- 1 bay leaf
- 2 tablespoons olive oil
- 1/4 teaspoon freshly ground black pepper
- 2 cups dried cannellini or other white beans, soaked, rinsed, drained
- 6 cups water
- 1/2 teaspoon salt, divided

Directions:

1. In a large frying pan, heat the olive oil over medium heat to create the croutons. Sauté for 1 minute after adding the garlic.
2. Remove the pan from the heat and let aside for 10 minutes to allow the garlic taste to permeate the oil. Remove and discard the garlic cloves.
3. Return the pan to a medium-high heat setting.
4. Add the bread cubes and cook, turning regularly, for 3 to 5 minutes, or until gently browned. Place the mixture in a small basin and set it aside.
5. To create the soup, put the white beans, water, 1/4 teaspoon salt, and bay leaf in a soup pot. Over high heat, bring to a boil.
6. Reduce the heat to low, partially cover, and cook for 60 to 75 minutes, or until the beans are cooked. Reserve 1/2 cup of the cooking liquid after draining the beans.
7. Remove the bay leaf and toss it out. Place the cooked beans in a large mixing basin and set aside the cooking pot.
8. Combine the saved cooking liquid and 1/2 cup of the cooked beans in a small bowl. To make a paste, mash with a fork.

9. Toss the cooked beans with the bean paste.
10. Add the olive oil to the cooking pot and return it to the fire. Heat to a medium-high temperature.
11. Stir in the onion and carrots and cook for 6 to 7 minutes, or until the carrots are tender-crisp.
12. Cook, stirring constantly, until the garlic is softened, about 1 minute.
13. Combine the remaining 1/4 teaspoon salt, pepper, rosemary, bean mixture, and stock in a mixing bowl.
14. Bring to a boil, then reduce to a low heat and continue to cook for 5 minutes, or until the stew is thoroughly heated.
15. To serve, ladle the stew into hot bowls and top with croutons.
16. Serve immediately with a rosemary twig garnishing each bowl.

Per serving: Calories: 307 Kcal; Fat: 7 g; Carbs: 45 g; Protein: 16 g: Sodium: 334 mg; Sugar: 3 g

168. Vegetable, Lentil and Garbanzo Bean Stew

Preparation time: 15 minutes

Cooking time: 1 hour

Servings: 8

Ingredients:

- 1 teaspoon turmeric
- 1/4 teaspoon saffron
- 3 cups butternut squash, peeled, seeded and cut into 1-inch cubes
- 3 garlic cloves, minced
- 4 cups low-sodium vegetable stock
- 1 can garbanzo beans, drained and rinsed
- 3 large carrots, peeled and cut into 1/2-inch pieces
- 1/2 cup chopped fresh cilantro
- 2 teaspoons ground cumin
- 1 teaspoon freshly ground pepper

- 1/4 cup lemon juice
- 2 large onions, chopped
- 1 cup red lentils
- 2 tablespoons no-added-salt tomato paste
- 2 tablespoons peeled and minced fresh ginger
- 1/2 cup chopped roasted unsalted peanuts

Directions:

1. Slowly sweat veggies (squash, carrots, onions, and garlic) in a Dutch oven over low to medium heat until onions begin to brown.
2. Scrape up the browned chunks of veggies from the bottom of the pan with the vegetable stock.
3. Combine the lentils, tomato paste, and seasonings in a large mixing bowl.
4. Cover and simmer over medium-low heat for 1 to 1 1/2 hours, or until lentils and squash are tender. Stir the mixture occasionally.
5. Alternatively, transfer the ingredients to a slow cooker and cook on low for 4-6 hours.
6. Combine the lemon juice and garbanzo beans in a mixing bowl.
7. Serve hot with chopped peanuts and cilantro on top.

Per serving: Calories: 287 Kcal; Fat: 7 g; Carbs: 41 g; Protein: 13 g: Sodium: 258 mg; Sugar: 0 g

169. Sweet Pepper Stew

Preparation time: 20 minutes

Cooking time: 50 minutes

Servings: 2

Ingredients:

- 1 cup low-sodium tomato juice
- 1 cup low-sodium vegetable stock
- 2 tablespoons olive oil
- ¼ cup brown lentils
- Salt, to taste
- 1 tablespoon gluten-free Worcestershire sauce
- 1 teaspoon oregano
- 2 sweet peppers, diced
- ½ large onion, minced
- 1 garlic clove, minced
- ¼ cup brown rice

Directions:

1. Heat the olive oil in a Dutch oven over medium-high heat.
2. Sauté the sweet peppers and onion for 10 minutes, or until the onion becomes golden and the peppers are wilted, turning periodically.
3. Cook for another 30 seconds after adding the garlic, Worcestershire sauce, and oregano.
4. Stir together the tomato juice, vegetable stock, rice, and lentils in the Dutch oven.
5. Bring the mixture to a boil, and then decrease to a medium-low heat setting.
6. Cover and cook for 45 minutes, or until the rice is soft and the lentils are cooked through.

Per serving: Calories: 378 Kcal; Fat: 15.6 g; Carbs: 52.3 g; Protein: 11 g: Sodium: 391 mg; Sugar: 4.2 g

170. Vegetable and Red Lentil Stew

Preparation time: 10 minutes

Cooking time: 35 minutes

Servings: 6

Ingredients:

- 4 celery stalks, finely diced
- 3 cups red lentils
- 1 teaspoon dried oregano
- 2 onions, peeled and finely diced
- 6½ cups water
- 1 tablespoon extra-virgin olive oil
- 2 zucchini, finely diced
- 1 teaspoon salt, plus more as needed

Directions:

1. In a large pot over medium heat, heat the olive oil.
2. Add the onions and cook, stirring constantly, for about 5 minutes, or until they are softened.
3. Bring the water, zucchini, celery, lentils, oregano, and salt to a boil in a large pot.
4. Reduce the heat to low and cover for 30 minutes, or until the lentils are cooked, stirring occasionally.
5. Season to taste and make any necessary adjustments.

Per serving: Calories: 387 Kcal; Fat: 4.4 g; Carbs: 63 g; Protein: 24 g: Sodium: 418 mg; Sugar: 4 g

171. Mediterranean Tomato Hummus Soup

Preparation time: 10 minutes

Cooking time: 10 minutes

Servings: 2

Ingredients:

- 1 cup roasted red pepper hummus
- Salt, to taste
- 1 can crushed tomatoes with basil
- 2 cups low-sodium chicken stock
- ¼ cup fresh basil leaves, thinly sliced, for garnish (optional)

Directions:

1. In a blender, puree the tinned tomatoes, hummus, and chicken stock until smooth.
2. Fill a pot halfway with water and bring to a boil. To taste, season with salt.
3. If preferred, serve with fresh basil on top.

Per serving: Calories: 147 Kcal; Fat: 6.2 g; Carbs: 20 g; Protein: 5.2 g: Sodium: 682 mg; Sugar: 4.9 g

172. Avgolemono (Lemon Chicken Soup)

Preparation time: 15 minutes

Cooking time: 60 minutes

Servings: 2

Ingredients:

- 1½ cups shredded rotisserie chicken
- ½ large onion
- ¼ cup brown rice
- 2 tablespoons chopped fresh parsley
- Salt, to taste
- 3 tablespoons freshly squeezed lemon juice
- 1 egg yolk
- 2 tablespoons chopped fresh dill
- 2 medium carrots
- 1 celery stalk
- 1 garlic clove
- 5 cups low-sodium chicken stock

Directions:

1. In a food processor, pulse the onion, carrots, celery, and garlic until the veggies are minced.
2. In a stockpot, combine the veggies and chicken stock and bring to a boil over high heat.
3. Remove from the fire and stir in the rice, shredded chicken, and lemon juice.
4. Cover and cook for another 40 minutes, or until the rice is tender.
5. Lightly whisk the egg yolk in a small bowl.
6. Slowly pour about a quarter of a ladle of broth into the egg yolk while whisking with one hand to warm, or temper, the yolk.
7. Continue to whisk as you slowly add another ladle of broth.
8. Turn off the heat and add the whisked egg yolk–broth combination to the soup pot. To blend, stir everything together thoroughly.
9. Toss in the dill and parsley.
10. Serve with a pinch of salt to taste.

Per serving: Calories: 172 Kcal; Fat: 4.2 g; Carbs: 16.1 g; Protein:18.2 g: Sodium: 232 mg; Sugar: 0.7 g

173. Vegetable Fagioli Soup Sugar

Preparation time: 30 minutes

Cooking time: 60 minutes

Servings: 2

Ingredients:

- 1 tablespoon olive oil
- 1 cup packed kale, stemmed and chopped
- 1 red kidney beans, drained and rinsed
- 1 can cannellini beans, drained and rinsed
- ½ cup chopped fresh basil
- Salt and freshly ground black pepper, to taste
- 1 large garlic clove, minced
- 3 tablespoons tomato paste
- 2 medium carrots, diced
- 2 medium celery stalks, diced
- ½ medium onion, diced
- 4 cups low-sodium vegetable broth

Directions:

1. In a stockpot, heat the olive oil over medium-high heat.
2. Sauté the carrots, celery, onion, and garlic for 10 minutes, or until the veggies have begun to turn golden.
3. Cook for about 30 seconds after adding the tomato paste.
4. Bring the soup to a boil with the veggie broth.
5. Reduce the heat to low and cover. Cook the carrots in the soup for 45 minutes, or until they are soft.
6. Purée the soup with an immersion blender until it is mostly smooth but still has some vegetable bits.
7. Combine the kale, beans, and basil in a large mixing bowl.
8. Serve after seasoning with salt and pepper to taste.

Per serving: Calories: 217 Kcal; Fat: 4.2 g; Carbs: 36 g; Protein: 10.2 g: Sodium: 482 mg; Sugar: 7.3 g

174. Chicken and Pastina Soup

Preparation time: 5 minutes

Cooking time: 20 minutes

Servings: 6

Ingredients:

- 1 tablespoon extra-virgin olive oil
- ¼ teaspoon kosher or sea salt
- 8 cups no-salt-added chicken or vegetable broth
- 3 cups packed chopped kale, center ribs removed
- 1 cup minced carrots
- 3 tablespoons grated Parmesan cheese
- ¾ cup uncooked acini de pepe or pastina pasta
- 2 cups shredded cooked chicken
- ¼ teaspoon freshly ground black pepper
- 2 garlic cloves, minced

Directions:

1. Heat the oil in a large stockpot over medium heat. Cook, stirring constantly, for 30 seconds after adding the garlic. Cook for 5 minutes, stirring periodically, after adding the kale and carrots.
2. Turn the heat to high and add the broth, salt, and pepper. Bring the stock to a boil before stirring in the pasta.
3. Reduce the heat to medium and cook for 10 minutes, or until the pasta is cooked through, tossing occasionally to prevent the spaghetti from sticking to the bottom of the pan.
4. Cook for another 2 minutes to warm the chicken thoroughly.
5. Divide the soup among six bowls. Serve with 12 tablespoons of cheese on top of each.

Per serving: Calories: 275 Kcal; Fat: 19 g; Carbs: 11 g; Protein: 16 g: Sodium: 298 mg; Sugar: 0.3 g

175. Mushroom Barley Soup

Preparation time: 5 minutes
Cooking time: 20 minutes
Servings: 6
Ingredients:

- 1 cup uncooked pearled barley
- ¼ cup red wine
- 2 tablespoons extra-virgin olive oil
- 6 cups no-salt-added vegetable broth
- 2 tablespoons tomato paste
- 1 cup chopped carrots
- 1 dried bay leaf
- 6 tablespoons grated Parmesan cheese
- 1 cup chopped onion
- 5½ cups chopped mushrooms
- 4 sprigs fresh thyme or ½ teaspoon dried thyme

Directions:

1. Heat the oil in a large stockpot over medium heat. Cook for 5 minutes, stirring often, after adding the onion and carrots. Add the mushrooms and increase the heat to medium-high. Cook, stirring often, for 3 minutes.
2. Combine the broth, barley, wine, tomato paste, thyme, and bay leaf in a large mixing bowl. Bring the soup to a boil, stirring occasionally. When it reaches a boil, stir a few times, then reduce to medium-low heat, cover, and simmer for another 12 to 15 minutes, or until the barley is tender.
3. Remove the bay leaf and ladle the soup into bowls, topping each with 1 spoonful of cheese.

Per serving: Calories: 195 Kcal; Fat: 4 g; Carbs: 34 g; Protein: 7 g: Sodium: 173 mg; Sugar: 3.1 g

176. Greens, Fennel, and Pear Soup with Cashews

Preparation time: 15 minutes
Cooking time: 15 minutes
Servings: 4
Ingredients:

- 2 pears, peeled, cored, and cut into ½-inch cubes
- 2 tablespoons olive oil
- 1 fennel bulb, cut into ¼-inch-thick slices
- 2 cups packed blanched spinach
- 3 cups low-sodium vegetable soup
- 2 leeks, white part only, sliced
- 1 teaspoon sea salt
- ¼ teaspoon freshly ground black pepper
- ½ cup cashews

Directions:

1. In a stockpot, heat the olive oil over high heat until it shimmers.
2. Add the fennel and leeks and cook for 5 minutes, or until the vegetables are soft.
3. Add the pears and season with salt and pepper, then cook for an additional 3 minutes, or until tender.
4. Combine the cashews, spinach, and vegetable soup in a mixing bowl. Bring the water to a boil. Reduce the heat to a low setting. Cover and cook for 5 minutes on low heat.
5. Place the soup in a food processor and pulse until smooth and creamy.
6. Return the soup to the pot and cook over low heat until well heated.
7. Immediately transfer the soup to a large serving bowl and serve.

Per serving: Calories: 266 Kcal; Fat: 15.1 g; Carbs: 32.9 g; Protein: 5.2 g: Sodium: 628 mg; Sugar: 12 g

177. Moroccan Lentil, Tomato, and Cauliflower Soup

Preparation time: 15 minutes
Cooking time: 4 hours
Servings: 6
Ingredients:

- 1 teaspoon extra-virgin olive oil
- ¼ cup chopped fresh cilantro
- ½ teaspoon ground coriander
- 1 cup dry lentils
- 28 ounces tomatoes, diced, reserve the juice
- 1½ cups chopped cauliflower
- 1 cup chopped carrots
- 1 cup chopped onions
- 3 cloves garlic, minced
- 1 cup chopped fresh spinach
- 1 teaspoon ground turmeric
- ¼ teaspoon ground cinnamon
- ¼ teaspoon freshly ground black pepper
- 4 cups low-sodium vegetable soup
- 1 teaspoon ground cumin
- 1 tablespoon no-salt-added tomato paste
- 1 tablespoon red wine vinegar (optional)

Directions:

1. Toss the carrots and onions with the minced garlic, coriander, cumin, turmeric, cinnamon, and black pepper in the slow cooker.
2. Stir everything together thoroughly.
3. Pour the vegetable soup and tomato paste over the lentils, tomatoes, and cauliflower. Drizzle with extra virgin olive oil. Stir everything together thoroughly.
4. Cover the slow cooker and simmer for 4 hours on high, or until the vegetables are cooked.
5. Open the top and stir the soup for the remaining 30 minutes of simmering time, then mix in the spinach.
6. In a large serving bowl, pour the cooked soup, top with cilantro, and drizzle with vinegar. Serve right away.

Per serving: Calories: 131 Kcal; Fat: 2.1 g; Carbs: 25 g; Protein: 5.6 g: Sodium: 364 mg; Sugar: 5.9 g

178. Carrot Soup

Preparation time: 25 minutes
Cooking time: 30 minutes
Servings: 6
Ingredients:

- 3 tablespoons all-purpose (plain) flour
- 1/4 teaspoon ground black pepper
- 10 carrots, scraped and sliced
- 1/4 teaspoon ground nutmeg
- 4 cups fat-free milk
- 2 tablespoons chopped fresh parsley
- 1 1/2 tablespoons sugar
- 2 cups water

Directions:

1. Heat the carrots, sugar, and water in a large pot.
2. Cover and cook for 20 minutes, or until the carrots are soft.
3. Drain and set aside part of the juice from the carrots. Remove from the equation.
4. Whisk together flour, pepper, nutmeg, and milk in a separate saucepan over medium-high heat.
5. Cook until the white sauce thickens, stirring continuously.
6. Combine the cooked carrots and white sauce in a blender or food processor.
7. Puree until completely smooth. To achieve the appropriate consistency, add the reserved liquid.
8. Pour into individual dishes and top with 1 teaspoon parsley. Serve right away.

Per serving: Calories: 124 Kcal; Fat: 0.1 g; Carbs: 24 g; Protein: 7 g: Sodium: 140 mg; Sugar: 11.1 g

179. Curried Cream of Tomato Soup with Apples

Preparation time: 20 minutes
Cooking time: 40 minutes
Servings: 8
Ingredients:

- 1 bay leaf
- 1/2 teaspoon thyme
- Ground black pepper, to taste
- 2 tablespoons olive oil
- 1 1/2 cups finely chopped onion
- 1 1/2 cups apple cubes
- 1 tablespoon curry powder, or to taste
- 3 cups no-salt-added canned tomatoes, drained
- 1 cup long-grain brown rice
- 1 cup finely chopped celery
- 1 teaspoon minced garlic
- 6 cups low-sodium vegetable or chicken broth
- 1 cup fat-free milk

Directions:

1. Heat the oil in a soup pot over medium heat. Add the chopped onion, celery, and garlic.
2. Cook for about 4 minutes, or until the vegetables are soft. Cook for 1 minute while tossing in the curry powder.
3. Combine the tomatoes, bay leaf, thyme, black pepper, and rice in a large mixing bowl. While heating to a boil, keep stirring regularly.
4. Pour in the broth. Return to a boil, then reduce to a low heat for around 30 minutes. Remove the bay leaf when the rice is tender.
5. Fill a food processor or blender halfway with soup and purée until smooth.

6. Return the soup to the pot and stir in the apple cubes and milk.
7. Cook until well heated. Immediately ladle into warmed individual bowls and serve.

Per serving: Calories: 205 Kcal; Fat: 5 g; Carbs: 32 g; Protein: 8 g: Sodium: 89 mg; Sugar: 6.7 g

180. Home-Style Turkey Soup

Preparation time: 25 minutes
Cooking time: 2 hours
Servings: 10
Ingredients:

For the broth:

- 1 turkey carcass
- 4 cups water
- 8 cups low-sodium chicken broth
- 3 large onions, 1 quartered and 3 chopped

For the soup:

- 1 bay leaf
- 1/2 teaspoon ground black pepper
- 1 onion, chopped
- 1/2 pound leftover light turkey meat, cut into bite-size chunks
- 1 cup diced rutabaga or turnip, peeled
- 1 cup chopped celery
- 1/4 cup chopped fresh parsley
- 1/4 teaspoon dried thyme
- 1 can white beans, rinsed and drained
- 4 carrots, peeled and cut into thin strips
- 1/4 cup uncooked pearl barley
- 1 can unsalted tomatoes

Directions:

1. Combine the turkey carcass, water, broth, and quartered onion in a large stockpot. Over high heat, bring to a boil.
2. Reduce the heat to low, cover, and cook for 1 hour.
3. Remove the carcass and onion from the stew and strain it.

4. Refrigerate the liquid — preferably overnight — and skim the fat from the surface of the soup.

5. Toss the liquid back into the stockpot.

6. Toss the soup ingredients into the broth.

7. Bring to a low simmer and cook for 1 hour, covered.

8. Immediately ladle into individual bowls and serve.

Per serving: Calories: 178 Kcal; Fat: 2 g; Carbs: 25 g; Protein: 15 g: Sodium: 131 mg;   Sugar: 5   g

Chapter 10: Desserts

181. Healthy Chocolate Chip Cookies

Preparation time: 10 minutes

Cooking time: 6 minutes

Servings: 16

Ingredients:

- 3/4 cups flour
- 1/4 teaspoon baking soda
- 3 oz. semi-sweet chocolate
- 2 tablespoons light butter softened
- 1/2 cup brown sugar
- 1/8 teaspoon salt
- 1 egg white beaten
- Chocolate chips
- 2 teaspoons vanilla extract

Directions:

1. Preheat oven to 350 degrees Fahrenheit.
2. Combine the butter, oil, and sugar in a medium mixing basin. Combine the vanilla, salt, and egg white in a mixing bowl.
3. Combine the flour and baking soda in a small bowl.
4. Mix in the flour mixture with the wet ingredients until the batter is smooth and lump-free.
5. Mix in the chocolate chips until everything is well combined.
6. Cook for 6-8 minutes or until golden brown, spooning the batter onto a prepared baking sheet.

Per serving: Calories: 76 Kcal; Fat: 2.3 g; Carbs: 12.6 g; Protein: 1.1 g: Sodium: 46.2 mg; Sugar: 7.8 g

182. Sugar Cookie

Preparation time: 15 minutes

Cooking time: 5 minutes

Servings:

Ingredients:

- 2 eggs, large
- 0.5 tsp sodium-free baking soda
- 1 tsp vanilla extract
- 4 cup all-purpose flour
- 1/2 cup butter, unsalted
- 2 cup baking blend Sweetener with Sugar
- 2 tbsp milk, buttermilk, fluid, cultured

Directions:

1. Preheat the oven to 375 degrees Fahrenheit.
2. Truvia blend cream margarine and shortening Mix in the eggs thoroughly.
3. Mix in the vanilla extract thoroughly.
4. Add baking soda to buttermilk in a small cup.
5. Allow it sit for one minute before adding to the egg mixture and combining thoroughly.
6. Blend the flour into the egg mixture thoroughly. Allow dough to chill for 2 hours. Roll out the dough to the proper thickness and use a cookie cutter to cut it out. Cookies should be placed on a baking pan.
7. Preheat oven to 350°F and bake for 5-7 minutes
8. Because the cookies will not brown, be careful not to over bake them.
9. Place the cookies on cooling racks.
10. Store in a firmly sealed container, covered. One cookie is a serving size.

Per serving: Calories: 193.41 Kcal; Fat: 8.45 g; Carbs: 32.01 g; Protein: 2.76 g; Sodium: 9.29 mg; Sugar: 11 g

183. Strawberries with Peppered Balsamic Drizzle

Preparation time: 1 hour 5 minutes

Cooking time: minutes

Servings: 4

Ingredients:

- 1 tablespoon brown sugar
- 2 cups fresh strawberries, washed and cut in half
- 1 tablespoon balsamic vinegar
- 4 ounces vanilla Greek yogurt
- Fresh mint, for garnish
- Pinch freshly and finely ground black pepper

Directions:

1. Combine the strawberries, balsamic vinegar, sugar, and pepper in a mixing bowl.
2. To make sure the berries are evenly coated, gently stir them in.
3. Set aside for 1 hour at room temperature, then refrigerate until ready to serve.
4. Place a spoonful of yoghurt on top of each strawberry in each of four bowls. Serve with a sprig of fresh mint as a garnish.

Per serving: Calories: 65 Kcal; Fat: 2 g; Carbs: g; 0Protein: 3 g: Sodium: 15 mg; Sugar: 0 g

184. Vanilla Chia Seed Pudding Toppings

Preparation time: 5 minutes (4 hours for freezing)

Cooking time: 0 minutes

Servings: 10

Ingredients:

- 2 cups reduced-fat 2 percent milk
- 1/2 cup chia seeds
- 1 cup vanilla Greek yogurt
- 1-1/2 tablespoons maple syrup
- 1/2 teaspoon vanilla extract

Directions:

1. Whisk together the yoghurt, milk, chia seeds, maple syrup, vanilla, and salt in a large mixing bowl until well combined.
2. Refrigerate for 3 to 4 hours or overnight, covered. If necessary, whisk again when ready to serve to smooth out any clumps that may have developed.
3. Fill dessert cups halfway with the mixture and top with your chosen toppings

Per serving: Calories: 92 Kcal; Fat: 4 g; Carbs: 10 g; Protein: 5 g: Sodium: 49 mg; Sugar: 5 g

185. Mango Banana Soft Serve

Preparation time: 10 minutes (4 hours for freezing)

Cooking time: 0 minutes

Servings: 1

Ingredients:

- 1 to 2 tablespoons sugar
- 1-1/2 tablespoons lime juice
- 1 large ripe banana
- 1, 16-ounce package frozen mango chunks
- Mint leaves, for garnish
- 1, 1/2 tablespoons canned light coconut milk

Directions:

1. Peel the banana, cut it in half, and freeze it solid for at least 4 hours in a sealed freezer bag.
2. Combine the mango and sugar in a large mixing dish and set aside for 5 minutes. (Omit the sugar if you want a little more acidity.)
3. In a high-powered blender, combine the mango, banana, lime juice, and coconut milk and pulse for 3 to 4 minutes,

scraping down the sides with a tamper until the mixture is thick and smooth.

4. Spoon the soft serve into bowls and serve immediately for a softer texture, or freeze until ready to serve for a firmer texture. If desired, garnish with mint leaves.

Per serving: Calories: 85 Kcal; Fat: 1 g; Carbs: g; Protein: 1 g: Sodium: 3 mg; Sugar: 13.8 g

186. Almond and Apricot Biscotti

Preparation time: 30 minutes

Cooking time: 1 hour

Servings: 24

Ingredients:

- 2 tablespoons dark honey
- 1/2 teaspoon almond extract
- 3/4 cup whole-wheat (whole-meal) flour
- 2 tablespoons 1 percent low-fat milk
- 2 tablespoons canola oil
- 2/3 cup chopped dried apricots
- 1/4 cup coarsely chopped almonds
- 3/4 cup all-purpose (plain) flour
- 1/4 cup firmly packed brown sugar
- 1 teaspoon baking powder
- 2 eggs, lightly beaten

Directions:

1. Preheat the oven to 350 degrees Fahrenheit.
2. Combine the flours, brown sugar, and baking powder in a large mixing bowl.
3. To combine ingredients, whisk them together. Combine the eggs, milk, canola oil, honey, and almond extract in a mixing bowl.
4. Stir the dough with a wooden spoon until it barely starts to come together.
5. Add the apricots and almonds, chopped. Mix until the dough thoroughly using floured hands.
6. Shape the dough into a flattened log 12 inches long, 3 inches wide, and about 1

inch high on a long sheet of plastic wrap by hand.

7. Invert the dough onto a nonstick baking sheet by lifting the plastic wrap. Bake for 25 to 30 minutes, or until lightly browned.
8. Allow it cool for 10 minutes on another baking sheet. Preheat the oven to 350 degrees Fahrenheit.
9. On a cutting board, place the cooled log. Cut 24 1/2-inch broad slices crosswise on the diagonal using a serrated knife.
10. Arrange the slices on the baking sheet, cut-side down.
11. Return to the oven and bake for 15 to 20 minutes, or until crisp.
12. Allow to cool completely before transferring to a wire rack. Keep the container sealed.

Per serving: Calories: 75 Kcal; Fat: 2 g; Carbs: 12 g; Protein: 2 g: Sodium: 17 mg; Sugar: 6 g

187. Ambrosia with Coconut and Toasted Almonds

Preparation time: 20 minutes

Cooking time: 20 minutes

Servings: 8

Ingredients:

- 5 oranges, segmented
- 2 red apples, cored and diced
- 1/2 cup slivered almonds
- 1/2 cup unsweetened shredded coconut
- 1 small pineapple, cubed (about 3 cups)
- 2 tablespoons cream sherry
- Fresh mint leaves for garnish
- 1 banana, halved lengthwise, peeled and sliced crosswise

Directions:

1. Preheat the oven to 325 degrees Fahrenheit.

2. Spread the almonds out on a baking sheet and bake for 10 minutes, stirring regularly, until brown and fragrant.
3. Immediately transfer to a plate to cool. Bake for about 10 minutes stirring frequently, until the coconut is lightly toasted..
4. Immediately transfer to a plate to cool.
5. Combine the pineapple, oranges, apples, banana, and sherry in a large mixing basin.
6. Toss lightly to combine. Using individual bowls, divide the fruit mixture evenly.
7. The roasted almonds and coconut should be equally distributed, and the mint should be garnished. Serve right away.

Per serving: Calories: 177 Kcal; Fat: 5 g; Carbs: 30 g; Protein: 3 g: Sodium: 2 mg; Sugar: 12 g

188. Fruitcake

Preparation time: 40 minutes

Cooking time: 1 hour

Servings: 12

Ingredients:

- 1/4 cup sugar
- 1/2 cup rolled oats
- 1/2 cup unsweetened applesauce
- 1/2 cup crushed pineapple packed in juice, drained
- Zest and juice of 1 medium orange
- 1/2 teaspoon baking powder
- , dates or figs
- 1/2 cup unsweetened apple juice
- 2 tablespoons real vanilla extract
- 1/2 teaspoon baking soda
- 1 egg
- 1/2 cup crushed or chopped walnuts
- Zest and juice of 1 lemon
- 1/4 cup flaxseed flour
- 1 cup whole-wheat pastry flour

- 2 cups assorted chopped dried fruit, such as cherries, currants

Directions:

1. Combine the dried fruit, applesauce, pineapple, fruit zests and juices, and vanilla in a medium mixing basin.
2. Allow to soak for 15 to 20 minutes.
3. Using parchment (baking) paper, line the bottom of a 9-inch-by-4-inch pan.
4. Whisk together sugar, oats, flours, baking soda, and baking powder in a large mixing dish. Stir together the fruit and liquid combination with the dry ingredients.
5. Combine the egg and walnuts in a mixing bowl.
6. Fill loaf pan halfway with batter and bake for 1 hour, or until toothpick inserted in center comes out clean.
7. Allow the fruitcake to cool in the pan for 30 minutes before removing it.

Per serving: Calories: 299 Kcal; Fat: 5 g; Carbs: 41 g; Protein: 5 g: Sodium: 117 mg; Sugar: 5 g

189. Strawberries and Cream Cheese Crepes

Preparation time: 25 minutes

Cooking time: 10 minutes

Servings: 4

Ingredients:

- 8 strawberries, hulled and sliced
- 4 tablespoons cream cheese, softened
- 2 tablespoons sifted powdered sugar
- 2 tablespoons caramel sauce, warmed
- 2 teaspoons vanilla extract
- 2 prepackaged crepes, each about 8 inches in diameter
- 1 teaspoon powdered sugar for garnish

Directions:

1. Preheat the oven to 325 degrees Fahrenheit. Using cooking spray, lightly coat a baking dish.

2. Using an electric mixer, combine the cream cheese until smooth in a mixing basin.
3. Mix in the powdered sugar and vanilla extract. Mix thoroughly.
4. 1/2 of the cream cheese mixture should be spread on each crepe, leaving a 1/2 inch border around the edges.
5. 2 tablespoons strawberries on top Roll up the dough and set it seam-side down in the baking dish.
6. Bake for about 10 minutes, or until lightly browned.
7. Crepes should be cut in half.
8. Place four individual serving dishes on the table.
9. Top each with 1/2 tablespoon caramel sauce and a dusting of powdered sugar.
10. Serve right away.

Per serving: Calories: 143 Kcal; Fat: 7 g; Carbs: 17 g; Protein: 3 g: Sodium: 141 mg; Sugar: 11 g

190. Strawberry Shortcake

Preparation time: 30 minutes
Cooking time: 15 minutes
Servings: 8
Ingredients:

- 1/4 cup trans-free margarine (chilled)
- 2 1/2 teaspoons low-sodium baking powder
- 1 tablespoon sugar
- 3/4 cup fat-free milk (chilled)
- 1 3/4 cups whole-wheat pastry flour, sifted
- 1/4 cup all-purpose (plain) flour, sifted

For the topping:

- 6 cups fresh strawberries, hulled and sliced
- 3/4 cup plain or vanilla fat-free yogurt

Directions:

1. Preheat the oven to 425 degrees Fahrenheit. Coat a baking sheet with nonstick cooking spray.
2. Re-sift the flours, baking powder, and sugar into a large mixing basin.
3. Cut the cooled margarine into the dry ingredients with a fork until the mixture looks like coarse crumbs. Stir in the cooled milk only until a wet dough forms.
4. Turn the dough out onto a greased work area and knead gently 6 to 8 times with floured hands until the dough is smooth and workable.
5. Roll the dough into a 1/4-inch thick rectangle with a rolling pin. Cut the cake into 8 squares.
6. Place the squares on the prepared baking sheet and bake for 10 to 12 minutes, or until golden.
7. Place each biscuit on a separate platter. 3/4 cup strawberries and 1 1/2 tablespoons yoghurt on top of each. Serve right away.

Per serving: Calories: 218 Kcal; Fat: 6 g; Carbs: 36 g; Protein: 5 g: Sodium: 75 mg; Sugar: 10 g

191. Soft Chocolate Cake

Preparation time: 20 minutes
Cooking time: 45 minutes
Servings: 1
Ingredients:

- 1 teaspoon salt
- 1 1/2 cups fat-free plain yogurt
- 2 eggs
- 2 teaspoons baking powder
- 2 cups sugar
- 1 3/4 cups all-purpose flour
- 2 teaspoons baking soda
- 1 cup freshly brewed hot coffee
- 1 1/2 teaspoons vanilla extract
- 3/4 cup cocoa powder

Directions:

1. Preheat the oven to 350 degrees Fahrenheit. Sift together the sugar, flour, cocoa powder, baking soda, baking powder, and salt in a medium mixing basin.
2. Add the yoghurt to a mixing bowl.
3. Alternate adding the dry ingredients and the eggs to the mixing bowl on low speed.
4. Slowly pour in the coffee and vanilla extract.
5. Continue to mix until the batter is completely smooth.
6. Coat two 8-inches round cake pans with nonstick spray and divide the batter evenly between them.
7. Bake for 30 to 35 minutes, or until a toothpick inserted in the center of the cakes comes out clean.

Per serving: Calories: 117 Kcal; Fat: 1 g; Carbs: 38 g; Protein: 2 g: Sodium: 34 mg; Sugar: 12 g

192.   Banana Cranberry and Oat Bars

Preparation time: 15 minutes

Cooking time: 40 minutes

Servings: 16

Ingredients:

- 2 tablespoon extra-virgin olive oil
- 2 medium ripe bananas, mashed
- ½ cup almond butter
- ½ cup maple syrup
- ¼ cup oat flour
- ¼ cup ground flaxseed
- ¼ teaspoon ground cloves
- ½ cup dried cranberries
- ½ teaspoon ground cinnamon
- 1 teaspoon vanilla extract
- 1½ cups old-fashioned rolled oats
- ½ cup shredded coconut

Directions:

1. Preheat the oven to 400 degrees Fahrenheit (205 degrees Celsius). Grease an 8-inch square pan with olive oil after lining it with parchment paper.
2. In a mixing dish, combine the mashed bananas, almond butter, and maple syrup. Stir everything together thoroughly.
3. Stir in the remaining ingredients until they are completely combined and the mixture is thick and sticky.
4. Using a spatula, spread the mixture evenly on the square pan, then bake for 40 minutes, or until a toothpick inserted in the center comes out clean.
5. To serve, take them out of the oven and cut them into 16 bars.

Per serving: Calories: 145 Kcal; Fat: 7.2 g; Carbs: 18.9 g; Protein: 3.1 g: Sodium: 3 mg; Sugar: 11.2 g

193.   Glazed Pears with Hazelnuts

Preparation time: 10 minutes

Cooking time: 20 minutes

Servings: 4

Ingredients:

- 1 cup apple juice
- 1 tablespoon grated fresh ginger
- ¼ cup chopped hazelnuts
- 4 pears, peeled, cored, and quartered lengthwise
- ½ cup pure maple syrup

Directions:

1. Place the pears in a saucepan with the apple juice. Over medium-high heat, bring to a boil, and then reduce to medium-low. Constantly stir.
2. Continue to cook, covered, for another 15 minutes, or until the pears are soft.
3. In a separate pot, mix the ginger and maple syrup. Over medium-high heat, bring to a boil. Stir the mixture constantly. Remove the syrup from the heat and set it aside in a small bowl until ready to use.

4. Using a slotted spoon, transfer the pears to a large serving bowl, then drizzle with syrup.
5. Sprinkle the hazelnuts on top of the pears and serve right away.

Per serving: Calories: 287 Kcal; Fat: 3.1 g; Carbs: 66.9 g; Protein: 2.2 g: Sodium: 8 mg; Sugar: 12 g

194. Pecan and Carrot Cake

Preparation time: 15 minutes

Cooking time: 45 minutes

Servings: 12

Ingredients:

- ½ cup coconut flour
- 1 teaspoon baking powder
- 1 teaspoon baking soda
- ½ cup coconut oil, at room temperature
- ⅛ teaspoon sea salt
- ½ cup chopped pecans
- 2 tablespoon coconut oil for greasing the baking dish
- 2 teaspoons pure vanilla extract
- 6 eggs
- ½ teaspoon ground nutmeg
- 1 teaspoon ground cinnamon
- 3 cups finely grated carrots
- ¼ cup pure maple syrup

Directions:

1. Preheat the oven to 350 degrees Fahrenheit (180 degrees Celsius). Coconut oil should be used to grease a 13-by-9-inch baking dish.
2. In a large mixing basin, combine the vanilla essence, maple syrup, and 1/2 cup coconut oil. Stir everything together thoroughly.
3. Crack the eggs into the mixing dish and beat them together thoroughly. Remove from the equation.
4. In a separate basin, combine the coconut flour, baking powder, baking soda, nutmeg, cinnamon, and salt. Stir everything together thoroughly.

5. Make a well in the center of the flour mixture and pour in the egg mixture. Stir everything together thoroughly.

Per serving: Calories: 340 Kcal; Fat: 20 g; Carbs: 40 g; Protein: 4 g: Sodium: 180 mg; Sugar: 11.9 g

195. Cherry Walnut Brownies

Preparation time: 10 minutes

Cooking time: 20 minutes

Servings: 9

Ingredients:

- ½ cup whole-wheat pastry flour
- ½ cup unsweetened dark chocolate cocoa powder
- 2 large eggs
- ½ cup plain Greek yogurt
- ½ cup sugar
- ½ cup chopped walnuts
- ½ cup honey
- ¼ cup extra-virgin olive oil
- 1 teaspoon vanilla extract
- 9 fresh cherries, stemmed and pitted
- Cooking spray
- ¼ teaspoon baking powder
- ¼ teaspoon salt

Directions:

1. Preheat the oven to 375 degrees Fahrenheit (190 degrees Celsius) and place the rack in the center. Using cooking spray, coat a square baking pan.
2. Whisk together the eggs, yoghurt, sugar, honey, oil, and vanilla in a large mixing basin.
3. Combine the flour, cocoa powder, baking powder, and salt in a medium mixing basin. Whisk the flour mixture into the egg mixture until all of the dry ingredients are well combined. Combine the walnuts and fold them in.
4. Pour the batter into the pan that has been prepared. Push the cherries into the batter in three rows, three to a row,

so that one is in the middle of each brownie when cut into squares.

5. Bake for 20 minutes, or until the brownies are just set. Remove from the oven and cool   for 5 minutes on a wire rack. Serve cut into nine squares.

Per serving: Calories: 154 Kcal; Fat: 6 g; Carbs: 24 g; Protein: 3 g: Sodium: 125 mg; Sugar: 12 g

196. Peanut Butter and Chocolate Balls

Preparation time: 45 minutes

Cooking time: 0 minutes

Servings: 15 balls

Ingredients:

- 2 tablespoons softened almond butter
- ¾ cup creamy peanut butter
- 1¾ cups maple syrup
- ¼ cup unsweetened cocoa powder
- ½ teaspoon vanilla extract

Directions:

1. Line a baking sheet with a parchment paper..
2. In a mixing dish, combine all of the ingredients.
3. Stir everything together thoroughly.
4. Divide the dough into 15 equal parts and roll each into a 1-inch ball.
5. Place the balls on the baking sheet and chill for at least 30 minutes before serving.

Per serving: Calories: 146 Kcal; Fat: 1 g; Carbs: 16.9 g; Protein: 4.2 g: Sodium: 70 mg; Sugar: g

197. Crispy Sesame Cookies

Preparation time: 5 minutes

Cooking time: 10 minutes

Servings: 16

Ingredients:

- 2 large eggs
- 1 cup hulled sesame seeds

- 8 tablespoons almond butter
- 1¼ cups flour
- 1 cup sugar

Directions:

1. Preheat the oven to 350 degrees Fahrenheit (180 degrees Celsius).
2. Toast the sesame seeds for 3 minutes on a baking sheet. Remove from the oven and set aside to cool.
3. In a mixing bowl, combine the sugar and butter. Add the eggs one at a time, mixing thoroughly after each addition. Mix in the flour and toasted sesame seeds until fully combined.
4. Drop spoonsful of cookie dough onto a baking sheet and roll into round walnut-like balls, about 1 inch in diameter.
5. Bake for 5 to 7 minutes, or until golden brown, in the oven.
6. Allow 5 minutes for the cookies to cool before serving.

Per serving: Calories: 218 Kcal; Fat: 12 g; Carbs: 25 g; Protein: 4 g: Sodium: 58 mg; Sugar: 3 g

198. Crunchy Almond Cookies

Preparation time: 5 minutes

Cooking time: 5-7 minutes

Servings: 6

Ingredients:

- 8 tablespoons almond butter
- 1 large egg
- 1½ cups all-purpose flour
- ½ cup sugar
- 1 cup ground almonds

Directions:

1. Preheat the oven to 375 degrees Fahrenheit (190 degrees Celsius). Line a baking sheet with parchment paper.
2. In a mixing bowl, combine the sugar and butter. Mix in the egg until everything is well blended. While the mixer is on

slow, alternately add the flour and ground almonds, 1/2 cup at a time.

3. Drop 1 spoonful of dough onto the baking sheet, spacing the cookies at least 2 inches apart.

4. Place the baking sheet in the oven and bake for 5 to 7 minutes, or until the edges of the cookies begin to brown.

5. Remove from the oven and set aside to cool for 5 minutes before serving.

Per serving: Calories: 604 Kcal; Fat: 36 g; Carbs: 63 g; Protein: 11 g: Sodium: 181 mg; Sugar: 4 g

199.   Frozen Mango Raspberry Delight

Preparation time: 5 minutes

Cooking time: 0 minutes

Servings: 2

Ingredients:

- 1 teaspoon honey
- 3 cups frozen raspberries
- 1 peach, peeled and pitted
- 1 mango, peeled and pitted

Directions:

1. In a blender, combine all of the ingredients and puree until smooth, adding water as needed.

2. If preferred, place in the freezer for 10 minutes to harden up. Chill or serve at room temperature.

Per serving: Calories: 276 Kcal; Fat: 17.5 g; Carbs: 60.3 g; Protein: 4.5 g: Sodium: 4 mg; Sugar: 11 g

200.   Orange Mug Cake

Preparation time: 10 minutes

Cooking time: 3 minutes

Servings: 2

Ingredients:

- 6 tablespoons flour
- 2 tablespoons sugar
- 2 tablespoons freshly squeezed orange juice
- ½ teaspoon orange extract
- 1 teaspoon orange zest
- 1 egg
- 2 tablespoons olive oil
- 2 tablespoons unsweetened almond milk
- ½ teaspoon baking powder
- Pinch salt
- ½ teaspoon vanilla extract

Directions:

1. In a small mixing bowl, combine the flour, sugar, orange zest, baking powder, and salt.

2. Whisk together the egg, olive oil, milk, orange juice, orange extract, and vanilla extract in a separate bowl.

3. Combine the dry and wet ingredients in a mixing bowl and stir to combine. It will be a thick batter.

4. Pour the mixture into two small mugs and set aside. Each mug should be microwaved individually. Microwaves vary, but small mugs should take approximately 60 seconds and one large mug should take about 90 seconds.

5. Allow for 5 minutes of cooling before serving.

Per serving: Calories: 303 Kcal; Fat: 1 g; Carbs: 32 g; Protein: g: Sodium: 118 mg;   Sugar: 11.9   g

30 Days Meal Plan

Days	Breakfast	Lunch	Dinner
Day 1	Marinara Poached Eggs	Southwest Shredded Pork Salad	Grilled Vegetable Sewers
Day 2	Grilled Basil Lemon Tofu Burgers	Vegetable and Red Lentil Stew	Vegetable, Lentil and Garbanzo Bean Stew
Day 3	Bulger Breakfast with Fruits	Beef Stew with Fennel and Shallots	Greens, Fennel, and Pear Soup with Cashews
Day 4	Smoked Salmon Avocado Toast	Shrimp & Nectarine Salad	Baked chicken and Wild Rice
Day 5	Quinoa Breakfast Bowls	Stir Fried Eggplant	Grilled Lemon Chicken
Day 6	Mediterranean Breakfast Eggs	Mushroom Barley Soup	Glazed Root Vegetables
Day 7	Overnight Oats with Raspberries	Cherry-Chicken Lettuce Wraps	Mediterranean Baked Fish
Day 8	Green Smoothie with 2 boiled eggs	Beef, Tomato, and Lentils Stew	Home-Style Turkey Soup
Day 9	Fig with Ricotta Oatmeal	Rustic Lentil and Basmati Rice Pilaf	Beef and Vegetable Stew

Day 10	Delicious Fluffy Almond Flour Pancakes	Slow Cook Lamb Shanks with Cannellini Beans Stew	Gyro Burgers with Tahini Sauce
Day 11	Morning Mediterranean Frittata	Turkey Medallions with Tomato Salad	Spiced Roast Chicken
Day 12	Vegetarian Breakfast Salad with Eggs	Asian Pork Tenderloins	Shrimp & Nectarine Salad
Day 13	Dried Cranberries Cinnamon Oatmeal	Italian Sausage-Stuffed Zucchini	Quick Chicken Salad Wraps
Day 14	Grilled Basil Lemon Tofu Burgers	Baked chicken and Wild Rice	Roasted Salmon with Maple Glaze
Day 15	Easy Berry and Nut Parfait	Sea Food Corn Chowder	Parsley-Dijon Chicken and Potatoes
Day 16	Cheesy Egg in Avocado	Warm Rice and Pinto Salad + Mexican Bake	Chicken and Pastina Soup
Day 17	Mediterranean Breakfast Eggs	Coconut Chicken Tenders	Grilled Vegetable Sewers
Day 18	Morning Overnight Oats with Raspberries	Thai-Style Cobb Salad + Almond Crusted Chicken Tenders with Honey	Beef and Vegetable Stew
Day 19	Dried Cranberries Cinnamon Oatmeal	Black Bean and Corn Relish	Honey-Mustard Roasted Salmon
Day 20	Savory Breakfast Oatmeal	Macadamia Pork	Cherry-Chicken Lettuce Wraps

Day 21	Bulger Breakfast with Fruits	Grilled Chicken and Zucchini Kebabs	Roasted Pork Tenderloin
Day 22	Corn Banana Fritters	Black Bean & White Cheddar Frittata	Greek-Style Lamb Burgers
Day 23	Baked Avocado Eggs	Curried Cream of Tomato Soup with Apples + Spiced Citrus Sole	Salmon and Mushroom Hash with Pesto
Day 24	Smoked Salmon Avocado Toast	Salmon with Horseradish Pistachio Crust	Home-Style Turkey Soup
Day 25	Simple Apple Tahini Toast	Turkish Canned Pinto Bean Salad + Crispy Pesto Chicken	Seasoned Baked Cod
Day 26	Morning Mediterranean Frittata	Five-spice pork medallions	Southwest Shredded Pork Salad
Day 27	Vegetarian Breakfast Salad with Eggs	Beef stroganoff	Lamb Kofta (Spiced Meatballs
Day 28	Delicious Fluffy Almond Flour Pancakes	Pesto Corn Salad with Shrimp	Crispy Tilapia with Mango Salsa
Day 29	Green Smoothie with 2 boiled eggs	Crab Cake Egg Stacks	Beef and Vegetable Kebabs
Day 30	Fig with Ricotta Oatmeal	Rustic Lentil and Basmati Rice Pilaf	Cilantro Lime Shrimp + Baby Potato and Olive Salad

Measurement Conversion Chart

Cups	Fluid Ounces	Tablespoons	Teaspoons
1	8	16	48
2/4	6	12	36
½	4	8	24
1/3	2 2/3	5 tbsp. + 1 tsp	16
¼	2	4	12
1/16	0.5	1	3

INDEX

A

Acorn squash with Apples; 54
Almond and Apricot Biscotti; 104
Ambrosia with Coconut and Toasted Almonds; 104
Asian Pork Tenderloin; 78
Asparagus with Hazelnut Gremolata; 54
Asparagus with Horseradish Dip; 34
Avgolemono (Lemon Chicken Soup); 96
Avocado Dip; 35
Avocado Salsa; 36

B

Baby Minted Carrots; 56
Baby Potato and Olive Salad; 32
Baked Apples with Cherries and Almonds; 55
Baked Avocado Eggs; 22
Baked chicken and Wild Rice; 78
Baked Halibut Steaks with Vegetables; 76
Baked Lemon Salmon; 73
Baked Salmon with Basil and Tomato; 73
Banana Cranberry and Oat Bars; 107
Bean Salad with Balsamic Vinaigrette; 44
Beef and Vegetable Kebabs; 86
Beef and Vegetable Stew; 93
Beef Stew with Beans and Zucchini; 91
Beef Stew with Fennel and Shallots; 92
Beef stroganoff; 87
Beef, Tomato, and Lentils Stew; 90
Black Bean & Sweet Potato Rice Bowls; 41
Black Bean & White Cheddar Frittata; 40
Black Bean and Corn Relish; 42
Black Bean Wrap; 45
Blue Cheese Dressing; 39
Braised Celery Root; 55
Braised Kale with Cherry Tomatoes; 56
Broccoli with Garlic and Lemon; 57
Brussels sprouts with Shallots and Lemon; 65
Bulgur Breakfast with Fruits; 16

C

Cannellini Bean Hummus; 40
Carrot Soup; 99
Cauliflower Hash with Carrots; 52
Cauliflower Mashed 'Potatoes'; 57
Cauliflower Steaks with Arugula; 64
Celery and Mustard Greens; 60

Ch

Cheesy Baked Zucchini; 57
Cheesy Egg in Avocado; 16
Cherry Walnut Brownies; 108
Cherry-Chicken Lettuce Wraps; 28
Chicken and Pastina Soup; 97
Chickpea Lettuce Wraps with Celery; 66
Chickpea Mint Tabbouleh; 30
Chinese Style Asparagus; 61

C

Cilantro Lime Dressing; 36; 39
Cilantro Lime Shrimp; 32
Coconut Chicken Tenders; 87
Corn Banana Fritters; 21
Crab Cake Egg Stacks; 69
Creamy Cauliflower Chickpea Curry; 50
Creole Style Black Eyed Peas; 62
Crispy Pesto Chicken; 84
Crispy Sesame Cookies; 109
Crispy Tilapia with Mango Salsa; 75
Crunchy Almond Cookies; 109
Crunchy Baked Fish; 70
Crusted; 82
Curried Cream of Tomato Soup with Apples; 100

D

Dash Diet Waldorf Salad; 24
Delicious Fluffy Almond Flour Pancakes; 19
Dill Dip; 35
Dried Cranberries Cinnamon Oatmeal; 21

E

Easy Berry and Nut Parfait; 23
Edamame Salad with Sesame Ginger Dressing; 31
Eggplant with Toasted Spices; 63

F

Fig with Ricotta Oatmeal; 18
Five-spice pork medallions; 88
Frozen Mango Raspberry Delight; 110
Fruitcake; 105

G

Garlicky Zucchini Cubes with Mint; 52
Glazed Pears with Hazelnuts; 107
Glazed Root Vegetable; 64
Gluten-Free Hummus; 42
Greek-Style Lamb Burgers; 84
Green Beans with Red Pepper and Garlic; 64
Greens, Fennel, and Pear Soup with Cashews; 98
Grilled Basil Lemon Tofu Burgers; 18
Grilled Chicken and Zucchini Kebabs; 81
Grilled Lemon Chicken; 79
Grilled Romaine Lettuce; 65
Grilled Southwestern Steak Salad; 27
Grilled Vegetable Sewers; 59
Gyro Burgers with Tahini Sauce; 83

H

Healthy Avocado Smoothie; 22
Healthy Chocolate Chip Cookies; 102
Herbed-Mustard-Coated Pork Tenderloin; 80
Home-Style Turkey Soup; 100
Honey Sage Carrots; 59
Honey-Mustard Roasted Salmon; 74
Hot 6-Grain Cereal; 46
House Ranch Dressing; 36
Hummus; 43

I

Italian Salad Dressing; 36
Italian Sausage-Stuffed Zucchini; 29

L

Lamb Kofta (Spiced Meatballs); 85
Layered Hummus Dip; 34
Lentil Medley; 28
Lentil Ragout; 60
Low Carb Green Smoothie; 17
Low Sodium Spaghetti Sauce; 35

M

Macadamia Pork; 81
Mango Banana Soft Serve; 103
Mango Salsa; 37
Marinara Poached Eggs; 17
Mediterranean Baked Fish; 68
Mediterranean Breakfast Eggs; 19
Mediterranean Grilled Sea Bass; 76
Mediterranean Tomato Hummus Soup; 96
Mexican Bake; 40
Minestrone Soup; 49
Morning Mediterranean Frittata; 20
Morning Overnight Oats with Raspberries; 20

Moroccan Lentil, Tomato, and Cauliflower Soup; 99
Moroccan Tagine with Vegetables; 53
Mushroom Barley Soup; 98
Mushroom Sauce; 38

O

Orange Mug Cake; 110

P

Parsley-Dijon Chicken and Potatoes; 82
Peach Honey Spread; 37
Peanut Butter and Chocolate Balls; 109
Peanut Butter Hummus; 37; 43
Pecan and Carrot Cake; 108
Pepper Sauce; 37
Pesto Corn Salad with Shrimp; 30
Potato Lamb and Olive Stew; 90
Potato Salad; 60
Prawns Puttanesca; 70

Q

Quick Bean and Tuna Salad; 44; 71
Quick Chicken Salad Wraps; 79
Quick Spanish Rice; 47
Quinoa Breakfast Bowls; 17
Quinoa Risotto with Arugula and Parmesan; 71

R

Rainbow Slaw; 24
Rice and Beans Salad; 45
Roasted Chicken Thighs With Basmati Rice; 80
Roasted Pork Tenderloin; 85
Roasted Salmon; 72
Roasted Salmon with Maple Glaze; 72
Roasted Sweet Potato & Chickpea Pitas; 25
Roasted Veggies and Brown Rice Bowl; 49
Rustic Lentil and Basmati Rice Pilaf; 47

S

Salmon and Mushroom Hash with Pesto; 74
Salmon with Horseradish Pistachio Crust; 69
Sardines with Lemony Tomato Sauce; 32
Savory Breakfast Oatmeal; 22
Savory Vegetable Dip; 38
Sea Food Corn Chowder; 68
Seasoned Baked Cod; 73
Shrimp & Nectarine Salad; 24
Shrimp with Black Bean Pasta; 47
Simple Apple Tahini Toast; 22
Skinny Quinoa Veggie Dip; 34
Slow Cook Lamb Shanks with Cannellini Beans Stew; 91
Smoked Salmon Avocado Toast; 19

Soft Chocolate Cake; 106
Southwest Shredded Pork Salad; 31
Spiced Citrus Sole; 75
Spiced Roast Chicken; 86
Spicy Almonds; 29
Spicy Haddock Stew; 77
Spinach Dip with Mushrooms; 39
Stir Fried Eggplant; 66
Strawberries and Cream Cheese Crepes; 105
Strawberries with Peppered Balsamic Drizzle; 103
Strawberry Shortcake; 106
Strawberry-Blue Cheese Steak Salad; 25
Stuffed Portobello Mushrooms with Spinach; 51
Sugar Cookie; 102
Sweet Pepper Stew; 62; 95
Swiss Chard Egg Drop Soup; 49

T

Thai-Style Cobb Salad; 28
Turkey Medallions with Tomato Salad; 26
Turkish Canned Pinto Bean Salad; 46
Tuscan White Bean Stew; 93

V

Vanilla Chia Seed Pudding Toppings; 103
Vegetable and Red Lentil Stew; 63; 95
Vegetable and Tofu Scramble; 61
Vegetable Fagioli Soup Sugar; 97
Vegetable salsa; 38
Vegetable, Lentil and Garbanzo Bean Stew; 94
Vegetarian Breakfast Salad with Eggs; 16
Veggie-Stuffed Portobello Mushrooms; 51

W

Warm Rice and Pinto Salad; 26
White Bean Dip; 43
White Beans & Bow Ties; 41
Whole-Grain Pancakes; 44
Wilted Dandelion Greens with Sweet Onion; 59

Z

Zoodles; 61
Zucchini and Artichokes Bowl with Farro; 52
Zucchini Fritters; 53

Conclusion

Studies have shown that the DASH diet has been an easy and effective way to lower blood pressure and improve health. It can be used to prevent and treat hypertension and the complications caused by it.

A reduction in daily salt intake can lower blood pressure. No significant evidence has been found to indicate whether this will reduce the risk of hard health problems like heart disease. Cutting your daily salt intake to 3/4 teaspoon (1,500 mg) or less has not been linked to any hard health benefits.

If you are healthy, there is no reason to follow this diet. However, if you have high blood pressure or think you may be sensitive to salt, then the DASH diet might be a good choice.

Made in the USA
Middletown, DE
18 November 2022

15334419R00066